Canada's Monsters

by Betty Sanders Garner

Illustrations: James Simpkins
John MacLeod
Initials: Laura Piotrowski

Potlatch Publications
35 Dalewood Crescent, Hamilton,
Ontario L8S 4B5

©1976 by Potlatch Publications

Front cover painting by James Simpkins.

Back cover courtesy Bigfoot Information Center.

Table of Contents illustration of Lake Utopia Monster, Lake Utopia, N.B., courtesy New Brunswick Museum.

1SBN 0-919676-06-5

Printed in Canada
Richardson Bond & Wright Limited
Owen Sound, Ontario

**FOR MY HUSBAND ROBERT
AND SONS CHRISTOPHER,
KIMBERLY AND PHILLIP**

table of contents

IN THE BEGINNING . . .

IN THE BEGINNING . . .

DINOSAURS LIVED OVER SIXTY million years ago during the Age of Reptiles. They roamed the land and frequented lakes, rivers, estuaries and deltas. Every last one had become extinct long before the birth of man. Their existence would still be a secret but for the evidence they left behind. Bones, shells, tracks, and impressions have been found in the sand, mud, lime-ooze, and other material that covered them, and later became hardened rock.

Triceratops, Scolosaurus, Albertosaurus, Ornithominus, Anatosaurus, and *Stegosaurus* are only a few of the many, many ancient reptiles that roamed the land now called Canada. Of the four hundred species known to science, sixty-five have been collected from two areas on the Red Deer River, Alberta, one hundred and twenty miles southeast of Calgary; and above Drumheller. Skeletons and bones have also been found in Saskatchewan, and fragmentary remains in Nova Scotia and Bathurst Island, Northwest Territories. Footprints have been found along the Peace River in British Columbia.

The earliest dinosaur bones and footprints are over two hundred and fifteen million years old. These fossils tell us many things about how the prehistoric animals looked and behaved. We can only guess their most common colour, which is generally considered to have been dark green or brown, like their nearest relative today - the crocodile.

Some dinosaurs were plant-eaters and others flesh-eaters. Some walked on their hind legs and others on all fours. Some were light-limbed and swift, while others were heavy, broadbacked and clumsy. Some were protected by bony armour, but others had only thin skin. On some, the heads were very small; others, huge and surmounted by sharp horns. Still others had powerful jaws equipped with long sharp teeth. The brain was primitive and very small.

The first remains were discovered in 1874 by G.M. Dawson, the

geologist with Her Majesty's Boundary Commission, in the Morgan Creek district of Saskatchewan, and the Milk River region, near Comrey, Alberta. Beginning in 1897 valuable finds were also made in this area by the Geological Survey of Canada. These finds and others over the next three years finally climaxed in a very exciting period of history known as the Great Canadian Dinosaur Rush. From 1910 to 1917 the excitement and intense activity in western Canada, along the cliff-like banks of the Red Deer River, rivalled the famous Yukon Gold Rush, although only a few dozen people were involved instead of many thousands. The rich harvest of bones reaped during these seven years and in the succeeding sixty years have been shipped to museums in eastern Canada, the United States and Europe.

Why these ancient reptiles became extinct is one of the great mysteries of the world. Although some were hardly monsters in size, measuring a mere six feet, others were veritable giants eighty feet long weighing more than thirty tons. Today only the blue whale is known to rival these statistics, reaching over one hundred feet in length and one hundred and fifty tons in weight.

Dinosaurs, then, were Canada's Monsters of all the prehistoric yesterdays. They led the way for all the other monsters - real, or half-real - discovered in this book.

chapter one

SETTING THE SCENE

PEOPLE EVERYWHERE AND IN
every age have been fascinated by monsters. Monsters have peered up
from the unknown depths of oceans, frolicked in lakes and rivers, and
jumped out unexpectedly from wildernesses.

Stories about sea monsters reach far back into ancient times when
belief in gods, demigods and great beasts with supernatural powers was
at its height. So strong was the concept of sea monsters among the
Norse in early times, they went so far as to design their long ships to
look like firedrakes. With the head at the bow, tail at the stern, oars like
legs amidships, shields like scales and sails like wings, they presented a
terrifying spectacle. The sight of the ship alone, without the hairy
horde aboard, must have been enough to strike terror into the hearts
of enemies.

For the most part, early stories of mermaids, unicorns and dragons
can be dismissed as myths or mere figments of man's imagination. But
some stories, like the ones about the many-armed sea monster, *Kraken,*
and the gigantic whale, *Leviathan,* are bounded in fact.

In the sixteeth century Bishop Olaus Magnus of Sweden and later,
Bishop Erick Pontoppidan of Norway, wrote extensively about the
Kraken, and the *Leviathan.* The *Kraken* was described as being so huge
he could pluck a sailor from the crosstrees high in the rigging of a ship.
It was his habit to rise from the depths before mighty storms, bringing
with him shoals of fish. If sailors, greedy for the tremendous catch,
stayed too long and the *Kraken* breached, they, their catch and their
vessel would be overpowered and devoured.

The ancient *Kraken* lives today in the form of the squid, a very "real" monster. Its body is torpedo-shaped and tapers away to a slender tail. Inside the body there is a horny plate that is covered by a thick protective "mantle." The squid has two huge goggle eyes and a parrot-like beak for tearing apart its prey. It has ten long thin tentacles, two of which are much longer than the rest. On each tentacle there are three rows of sucker-like discs that grip like a vice. The squid entwines a tentacle about its prey, which it drags to the bottom of the sea and tears apart.

Squids can be one foot long or they can be veritable giants. In 1871, and for almost ten years thereafter, great squids appeared off the coast of Newfoundland and Labrador. They crawled onto the beaches where they were stranded and died. Ships made numerous sightings and there were reports of small fishing boats being attacked. Squids will attack anything that moves at a given speed, and that they take to be their prey.

In 1872, a giant squid was run ashore by heavy seas at Coomb's Cove, Newfoundland. It had attempted to save itself by adhering to a rock, but some fishermen dragged it to the beach. Its body measured ten feet in length, and one arm was forty-two feet long. According to one observer, R. T. Bennett of English Harbour, "the skin and flesh were 2.25 inches thick, and reddish inside as well as out. The suction cup was surrounded by a serrated edge, almost like the teeth of a handsaw."

In September, 1877, a monster devilfish, a variety of squid, was washed up alive on Catalina Beach, Trinity Bay, Newfoundland, after a terrible storm. The creature measured forty feet in length, the body being nine feet, six inches, and the rest tentacles. The arms, at the base, were seventeen inches across, and their length eleven feet. The eyes were huge; they had a diameter of eight inches. The creature was sent to a New York taxidermist for preparation before being exhibited in brine at St. John's. It would seem the taxidermist knew very little of such creatures. He put it together with all the limbs and eyes in the wrong places!

While the Coomb's Cove specimen was certainly the longest of this gathering of squids, it was by no means the largest. In November and December, 1878, two truly gigantic squids appeared in Newfoundland - one at Thimble Tickle and the other at Three Arms. The first was the largest; it is the biggest specimen ever accepted by science. Here is a description of its capture, written by Rev. Moses Harvey of St. John's, to *The Boston Traveller*:

On the 2nd day of November last, Stephen Sperring, a fisherman residing in Thimble Tickle was out in a boat with two other men; not far from the shore they observed some bulky object, and, supposing it might be part of a wreck, they rowed toward it . . . to their horror (they) found themselves close to a huge fish, having large glassy eyes, which was making desperate efforts to escape, and churning the water into foam by the motion of its immense arms and tail. It was aground and the tide was ebbing. From the funnel at the back of its head it was ejecting large volumes of water, this being its method of moving

backwards . . .

Finding the monster partially disabled, the fishermen plucked up courage and ventured near enough to throw the grapnel of their boat, the sharp flukes of which, having barbed points, sunk into the soft body. To the grapnel they had attached a stout rope which they had carried ashore and tied to a tree, so as to prevent the fish from going out with the tide . . . At length it became exhausted and as the water receded it expired.

The fishermen, alas! knowing no better, proceeded to convert it into dog's meat . . .

This squid's body measured twenty feet from beak to the end of its tail. One of the arms was as thick as a man's body and measured thirty-five feet. Accordingly the eyes must have been about eighteen inches across and the beak nine inches in diameter.

What was the reason for this seeming mass suicide by squids along the Labrador and Newfoundland shores? Some scientists have suggested they were driven to the surface from caves in the deep reefs by an earthquake or some such disturbance. Their disappearance, after the ten year period, could have been caused by some change in the ocean currents that altered the temperature of the water and drove away the fish upon which the squids feed. Even after the squids stopped appearing on the beaches, whalemen continued to find huge hunks of tentacle vomited by whales.

Sperm whales and giant squids are deadly enemies and engage in terrible, titanic battles. While the whales invariably emerge victorious, nearly all of them bear circular scars - up to ten centimetres in diameter - made by hooks on a squid's tentacles.

Another denizen of the deep which could have given rise to tales about multi-limbed monsters is the *Sea Blurber (Cyanea Capillata),* or giant jellyfish, which inhabits the North Atlantic, the Pacific and the Arctic Oceans. An Inuit hunter, John Malakai from western Greenland, took an oath that he saw a pink jellyfish that measured at least eight feet across its umbrella. Ensnared in its tentacles was a ten to fifteen foot shark-like fish. According to Inuit hunters, large stinging jellyfish such as this, with tentacles estimated at two hundred and seventy-five feet in length, are not uncommon in Arctic waters.

Many efforts have been made to weigh and measure massive jellyfish, but so far efforts have failed. These giant animals deflate rapidly and break apart easily when attempts are made to lift them from the water. They generally disintegrate before they can be handled ashore.

The *Leviathan* was believed by the early sailors to be so huge it needed a fish three miles long for food daily! Many men could stand in its eye socket and a horse and rider could gallop up and down its "swallow." Its bulk covered an area equal to three football fields and contained over four acres. Stories told how this monster would lie just beneath the surface. The unsuspecting sailor, thinking the bottom close, would cast anchor. The flukes would become fouled in the folds of the monsters hide, disturbing him, whereupon he would sound, taking the ship and all aboard to the bottom of the sea.

At other times the *Leviathan* came to the surface and basked in the sun. Sailors, mistaking him for an island, would "go ashore," light fires

and begin cooking meals. Aroused by this aggravation, the monster would immediately dive, dragging all hands with him.

Modern science tends to correlate *Leviathan* with the whale family. This is not surprising; it is not uncommon for the blue whale to reach one hundred feet in length! The world's record is one hundred and thirteen and a half feet long with a weight exceeding one hundred and fifty tons. At birth this whale measures nearly twenty-three feet in length and weighs four thousand, four hundred pounds.

The existence of giant saurians, or sea-serpents, is a very real possibility. Yet in the absence of tangible evidence such as a specimen, a skeleton or other remains, their existence cannot be accepted by science. Giant squids and jellyfish, devilfish, whales and whale-sharks - all these find a place in zoological manuals, but the sea-serpent, which has been seen many, many more times than these, is still largely considered imaginary.

We know that great creatures very like those described in sea monster stories actually lived in ancient seas. Fossilized skeletons have been found that are over two hundred million years old. From some of these skeletons - relatives of today's whales - we know that one kind of prehistoric whale looked like a sea-serpent. It had a long flexible tail which it whipped as it swam. This ancient whale had a skull much like a dog's, and had only two legs - at the front, each bearing five digits.

At the end of the Middle Ages, the whale was drawn with terrible fangs and claws, and was said to be six hundred feet long and three hundred feet wide. Early pictures also showed "waterspouts" on its head, which leads us to believe that whales were often mistaken for sea-serpents.

Whale skeletons were once considered a great exhibition attraction by showmen. One American even went so far as to mix the fossil bones of several extinct whales to make the skeleton of a monster one hundred and twelve feet long.

From time to time the bodies of basking-sharks have been washed ashore and mistaken for sea-serpents. The basking-shark is the largest fish in temperate waters, commonly measuring forty feet in length, and occasionally as much as fifty feet. (Another lengthy specimen of the dozen kinds of shark which inhabit Canadian waters is *Carcharodon carcharias* - the great white shark - which grows to forty feet. A fisherman sitting in a dory on St. Pierre Bank, south of Newfoundland, was visited by a great white; the species was identified by the teeth left behind on the badly scarred hull of the boat!) In spring and fall the dorsal fin of the basking-shark can be seen cutting through the ocean surface along Canadian coasts, most commonly in British Columbia. This fish mysteriously disappears in the fall.

In a state of decomposition, the great bulk of the basking-shark strongly resembles a sea-serpent, and looks as little as possible like his living self. The only bony structure he possesses is his back bone, which runs from the base of his small skull to the very tip of his tail. The vertebrae are held together by a covering of gristle; the rest of his body, apart from the gill-frames, is entirely flesh and soft cartilage. This quickly and easily breaks away in decomposition leaving only a skull, backbone and a little flesh adhering around the fins and tail. The long, bare expanse of backbone between the small head and the tail looks amazingly like the long, thin neck of a sea-serpent.

Basking-sharks have a habit of swimming in a line, one behind the other. Their dorsal and tail fins, rising high above the surface, have inspired many tales of living sea-serpents. In his book *Shark-O!* the British writer P. Fitzgerald O'Connor tells of seeing numerous basking-sharks "head to tail in one long sinuous line . . . as far as the eye could see and further . . . It seemed to us in that evening light, that some basic animal force was indeed at work - that every shark in the area must have been brought to this particular part of the coast at this particular hour by some irresistible urge in its being."

In 1938 the ancient coelacanth was dramatically discovered off the South African coast. This ancient fish, three feet long and weighing one hundred and twenty pounds, first lived three hundred million years ago and had long been considered extinct. If the coelacanth could survive from the ancient past, why not larger animals? Although the existence of such creatures has been known for hundreds of years, little is known of their habitats and lifestyles. But secrets are not difficult to keep in the sea, which reaches depths of more than thirty thousand feet.

Man has barely begun to explore the exciting and astonishing world of the sea; divers seldom descend below fifty fathoms, and then only on the continental shelf near the coast. They can know only a fraction of the sea's fauna. Who can say what strange and giant creatures exist buried deep in those mysterious depths? Unfortunately, carcases of sea monsters are seldom washed ashore; because of their enormous weight, they quickly sink to the bottom to be consumed by scavengers. And sightings of live specimens are no longer common. In the old days when movement upon the seas was by sail, ships covered greater areas, being forced to wander by winds and currents. Hence, there was a good chance of accidentally coming upon an unknown sea creature. Today's ships are power driven, and they stick to the shortest and quickest routes - the shipping lanes - and the creatures of the sea have learned to steer clear.

But belief in monsters of the deep persists. There is the *Skrimsl,* of Scandinavian folklore, a forty-six foot long monster that lives in a lake in Iceland. He is often seen in Thorska Fiord rocking on the surface of the water like a big boat floating with its keel in the air.

The *Loch Ness Monster,* the famous "waterhorse" of Scottish legend, is continuously in the news. Between twenty and forty feet long, it is most often sighted early in the morning and most frequently near Urquhart Castle. In 1960 the monster was even captured on film by Tim Dinsdale. Serious investigations are constantly being undertaken at the loch, as researchers try to prove once and for all that the *Loch Ness Monster* is *real.*

While the Britisher's pride in "Nessie" is, without doubt, justified, Canadians should be just as proud of their famous lake monster. His name is *Ogopogo,* and he lives in Lake Okanagan in the far west on the Pacific slopes of the Rockies. He is twenty to thirty feet long and has a heavy snake's body. *Ogopogo* has been part of Indian legend for centuries; their name for him is *Naitaka.*

Indian and Inuit folklore includes many monsters. There are gods and demigods who inhabit underground worlds and the depths of the seas. There are werewolves and werebears among Ojibway stories, and a horned water-serpent is prominent in Algonquin mythology.

Stories of monsters in human form are common amongst most tribes. The Micmac, near Chaleur Bay, New Brunswick, believe a fearful monster in the shape of a woman and as tall as the mast of a ship ate Indians and had a great hunting pouch in which to carry them. Another female man-eating semi-deity of the west coast was *Cannibal Woman.* According to accounts given by natives in 1890, a giant male cannibal named *Goo-teekhl* had terrorized the Tlingit villages of the Chilkat people for years by stealing children. Neither arrows nor spears would kill him. The woodlands people, as they moved alone through the forests, were fearful of encountering their cannibal giant *Windigo,* or *Weetigo.*

To the whiteman, most of these monsters remain little more than legends. The belief in *Windigo* was probably born out of the Ojibway and Cree Indian's fear of being driven to cannibalism by starvation. But there is considerable evidence to support the existence of the gigantic water-serpent *Hiachuckaluck,* and another monster - a wild, giant man-beast, known variously among the tribes as *Dsonoqua, Saskehavas, Smy-a-Likh, Omah, Bukwas, Seeahtik,* or *Sasquatch* - that lives in the deep forests of northwest British Columbia.

Do monsters really exist? Or are they merely extensions of Indian and Eskimo legends? Are they, perhaps, just products of man's overworked imagination?

The reader of this book will travel through the forests, mountain wildernesses, rivers, lakes and oceans of Canada in search of monsters, to examine and evaluate reports and testimonies of dozens of witnesses who claim actually to have *seen* them. He or she should not expect to find the answers to all the fascinating mysteries; nevertheless, it will be an exciting and incredible journey.

chapter two

SASQUATCH!

LONG BEFORE THE WHITE MAN'S first reported sightings, the Indians told about *Saskehavas,* who lived in the forests and mountains of the British Columbian northwest. Half-man and half-beast, this giant, hairy wildman stands from six to nine feet tall and weighs six hundred to nine hundred pounds. His head is apelike, with low brow and sloping forehead rising to a crest at the back of the skull. Walking upright like a man and taking six to eight foot strides, he leaves deep, human-like footprints from fourteen to twenty-two inches long. He is said to communicate by way of a high pitched whistling scream. And he is very shy of human contact.

Indian folk lore places the habitat of the *Sasquatch* mainly in the vicinity of Harrison Lake, B.C., sixty miles from Vancouver, but they have been reported as far inland as Kamloops. One report came from Greendrop Lake near Jasper, across the border in Alberta and hundreds of miles northeast of Harrison Lake country. Other reports, gathered in recent years, indicate these creatures are also known in the Yukon and even Labrador.

The Chehalis Indians of Harrison Lake area believe the *Sasquatch* are descendants of two bands of giants who were almost exterminated in battle many years ago. They are said to inhabit remote mountain caves and to meet periodically near the top of Morris Mountain. Stories tell of the *Sasquatch* kidnapping Indian maidens, stealing fish from house-wive's larders, hurling rocks at prospectors and killing deer with clubs.

Before the early 1800's a great number of sightings and even face-to-face encounters with *Sasquatch* went unrecorded. Witnesses

were afraid to tell about these sightings for fear of ridicule and cries of "hoax." Over the last one hundred and sixty years, however, sightings have been "documented" by white residents of the region, some as recently as the 1970's.

Since 1954, John Green, journalist and former owner of the *Agassiz-Harrison Advance,* has collected and recorded stories about the hairy wild giants. He has published three excellent books on the subject: *On the Track of the Sasquatch* (1968), *Year of the Sasquatch* (1970), and *The Sasquatch File* (1973).

The earliest written record of a belief in the *Sasquatch* is that of Alexander Caulfield Andersen, an officer of the Hudson's Bay Company. He established a post near Harrison Lake in 1846. His work was to explore and establish the most practical route for fur brigades to travel between the company's coastal posts, up the Fraser River and over the mountains into the interior. His reports frequently mentioned the wild giants and stated that the "hairy humanoids" had hurled rocks down on his party as they worked through the awesome Fraser River canyon.

The first public notice of such a creature appeared in the July 4th, 1884, edition of *The Daily British Colonist,* published at Victoria, B.C. On a regular train from Lytton to Yale, railroad men had actually captured a young *Sasquatch* found lying beside the tracks! Here is the report as it appeared:

WHAT IS IT?
A Strange Creature
Captured Above Yale.
A British Columbia Gorilla.

Yale, B.C. July 3, 1884 - In the immediate vicinity of No.4 tunnel, situated some twenty miles above this village, are bluffs of rock which have hitherto been insurmountable, but on Monday morning last were successfully scaled by Mr. Onderdonk's employees on the regular train from Lytton. Assisted by Mr. Costerton, the British Columbia Express Company's messenger, and a number of gentlemen from Lytton and points east of that place who, after considerable trouble and perilous climbing, succeeded in capturing a creature which may truly be called half man and half beast. "JACKO," as the creature has been called by his capturers, is something of the gorilla type, standing about four feet, seven inches in height and weighing 127 pounds. He has long, black strong hair and resembles a human being with one exception, his body, excepting his hands (or paws) and feet, is covered with glossy hair about one inch long. His forearm is much longer than a man's forearm, and he possesses extraordinary strength, as he will take hold of a stick and break it by wrenching or twisting it, which no man living could break in the same way.

Since his capture he is very reticent, only occasionally uttering a noise which is half-bark and half-growl. He is, however, becoming daily more attached to his keeper, Mr. George Telbury, of this place, who proposes shortly starting from

Photograph by Roger Patterson, courtesy Rene Dahinden.

London, England, to exhibit him. His favourite food so far is berries, and he drinks fresh milk with evident relish. By the advice of Dr. Hannington, raw meats have been withheld from Jacko, as the doctor thinks it would have a tendency to make him savage.

The mode of capture was as follows: Ned Austin, the engineer, on coming in sight of the bluff at the eastern end of the No.4 tunnel saw what he supposed to be a man lying asleep in close proximity to the track, and as quick as thought blew the signal to apply the brakes. The brakes were instantly applied, and in a few seconds the train was brought to a standstill. At this moment the supposed man sprang up, and uttering a sharp quick bark, began to climb the steep bluff. Conductor R. J. Craig and Express Messenger Costerton, followed by the baggageman and brakeman, jumped from the train and, knowing they were some 20 minutes ahead of the time, immediately gave chase. After five minutes of perilous climbing the then supposed demented Indian was corralled on a projecting shelf of rock where he could neither ascend or descend. The query now was how to capture him alive, which was quickly decided by Mr. Craig, who crawled on his hands and knees until he was about forty feet above the creature. Taking a small piece of loose rock, he let it fall and it had the desired effect of rendering poor Jacko incapable of resistance for a time at least. The bell rope was then brought up and Jacko was lowered to terra firma. *After firmly binding him and placing him in the baggage car, "off brakes" was sounded and the train started for Yale. At the station a large crowd who had heard of the capture by telephone from Spuzzum Flat were assembled, each one anxious to have the first look at the monstrosity, but they were disappointed, as Jacko had been taken off at the machine shops and placed in charge of his present keeper.*

The question naturally arises, how came the creature where it was first seen by Mr. Austin? From bruises about its head and body, and apparent soreness since its capture, it is supposed that Jacko ventured too near the edge of the bluff, slipped, fell, and lay where found until the sound of the rushing train aroused him. Mr. Thos. White and Mr. Gouin, C.E., as well as Mr. Major, who kept a small store about half a mile west of the tunnel during the past two years, have mentioned having seen a curious creature at different points between Camps 13 and 17, but no attention was paid to their remarks as people came to the conclusion that they. had either seen a bear or stray Indian dog. Who can unravel the mystery that now surrounds Jacko? Does he belong to a species hitherto unknown in this part of the continent, or is he really what the train men first thought he was, a crazy Indian?

Jacko was exhibited at Yale until the interest wore off; then, it would seem, he was allowed quietly to disappear and return to his own kind. This was probably the kindest thing that could have happened, even though his value to science would have been very great had studies been made before his release.

chapter three

SASQUATCH KIDNAPS A MAN!

AMONG THE MOST REMARKABLE *Sasquatch* stories is one told by a man named Albert Ostman of Fort Langley, B.C. He claims he was kidnapped by an old male *Sasquatch* on the British Columbian coast in 1924 and held captive for a week by a family of four of the creatures. Fearing ridicule and wishing to forget his experience as quickly as possible, Ostman did not report it until many years later. Here are excerpts from the long and detailed story he eventually wrote:

> I have always followed logging and construction work. This time I had worked over one year on a construction job, and thought a good vacation was in order. British Columbia is famous for lost gold mines. One is supposed to be at the head of Toba Inlet . . . why not look for this mine and have a vacation at the same time?

Arriving at Lund, Ostman gathered his equipment: a bedroll and camp gear, a prospector's pick and gold pan, a sheath knife, one 30-30 Winchester rifle and two boxes of shells, waterproof containers for matches, sugar and salt, and three rolls of snuff. His food consisted mostly of canned goods, a side of bacon, beans, prunes, macaroni, coffee and hardtack. He engaged an old Indian to take him to the head of Toba Inlet. On the way, the Indian entertained him with stories about the *Sasquatch*. Ostman said he did not believe the stories.

They reached the head of Toba Inlet and set up camp. The Indian ate supper with Ostman and then departed, promising to look out for him at the same place in about three weeks. Ostman spent seven days travelling, resting, prospecting and enjoying the beautiful scenery. He found a particularly good site near a spring and set up permanent camp.

That's when things began to happen. I am a heavy sleeper, not much disturbs me after I go to sleep. The next morning I noticed things had been disturbed during the night . . . but nothing (was) missing that I could see.

Ostman thought a porcupine had visited him during the night. The next night he was visited again, but this time a package of prunes and another of pancake flour were taken. Porcupines always look for salt, and since this was not touched he decided his visitor was something quite different. He didn't think it was a bear; they usually leave the place in a mess. He remained close to camp for the rest of the day in case his visitor should decide to return.

Before retiring that night Ostman took special notice of how things were arranged. He closed his packsack, hung it up and placed his pick near his bed. He took his shoes and rifle inside his sleeping bag and crawled in without undressing. Although he intended staying awake all night he fell asleep.

I was awakened by something picking me up. I was half asleep, and at first did not remember where I was . . . who ever it was, was walking. I tried to reason out what kind of animal this could be. I tried to get at my sheath knife, and cut my way out, but I was in an almost sitting position, and the knife was under me. I could not get hold of it, but the rifle was in front of me. I had a good hold of that. At times I could feel my packsack touching me, and . . . the cans in the sack touching my back.

After what seemed like an hour, I could feel we were going up a steep hill. What was carrying me was breathing hard and sometimes gave a slight cough. Now, I knew this must be one of the mountain Sasquatch *giants the Indian told me about.*

As nearly as Ostman could guess, he was carried for about three hours, uphill and downhill. Finally, he was dropped to the ground. He heard the rattle of the cans as his packsack was dropped beside him. He thrust his head out of the bag and filled his lungs with air. His legs felt too numb to move. In the darkness he could see little of his captors as they gathered around him, chattering excitedly. They did not touch him. Eventually he managed to crawl out of his sleeping bag and put on his shoes.

"What you fellows want with me?" he asked as he wobbled to his feet. But there was no answer.

As it grew lighter he could make out two large and two small

Jim McClarin's eight-foot statue of Bigfoot stands at Willow Creek, California. Shown with it is Rene Dahinden, who is five feet, nine inches tall.

creatures. They were covered all over with hair.

They looked like a family, old man, old lady and two young ones, a boy and a girl. The boy and girl seemed to be scared of me. The old lady did not seem too pleased about what the old man dragged home. But the old man was waving his arms and telling them all what he had in mind. They all left me then.

In his story, written many years later, Ostman described the "old man" as about eight feet tall, barrel-chested and with powerful shoulders and arms. His well proportioned forearms were longer than a man's. His hands were long and wide, and the palms were hollowed like scoops. His fingers were comparatively short and the fingernails were like chisels.

Ostman guessed that the "old lady's" age was between forty and seventy years, her height over seven feet and her weight about five hundred to six hundred pounds. Her hips were wide, and her walk was awkward and gooselike.

The young male was perhaps eleven to eighteen years old, seven feet tall, weighing approximately three hundred pounds. He had a narrow forehead which rose steeply four or five inches towards his crown.

The young female was smaller than her "brother" and was flat-chested.

Left alone, Ostman took stock of his situation. He was in a small valley or basin surrounded by high mountains. There was a V-shaped opening in the rocks on the southeast side, about eight feet wide at the bottom and flaring to twenty feet at the highest point. "That must be the way I came in," he told himself. "But how will I get out?"

The old man was now sitting as though guarding the opening. Obviously that was Ostman's only escape route. He decided, since the *Sasquatches* had not threatened him so far, that if he went about his business quietly and without fear they would be less likely to harm him. He picked up his rifle and pack and proceeded to set up camp in the shelter of two cypress trees, close to the west wall. In his packsack he found some tinned meat and vegetables, a can of coffee, three small cans of milk, hardtack, a sealer half-full of butter, a dozen matches and several small containers of snuff. He badly wanted a cup of coffee but had no utensils. He emptied the coffee into a dishtowel, filled the can with water from a nearby spring and eventually managed to brew himself a good hot drink.

The two young *Sasquatches* watched in fascination, from a distance. On the way back from the spring Ostman noticed where the family slept.

> *On the east side wall of this valley was a shelf in the mountain side, with overhanging rock, looking something like a big undercut in a big tree about ten feet deep and thirty feet wide. The floor was covered with lots of dry moss, and they had some kind of blankets woven with dry moss. They looked very practical and warm - with no need of washing.*

His first day with the *Sasquatches* passed uneventfully. The young male seemed very curious about the man, and as the day progressed, kept moving closer and closer. Finally, Ostman rolled an empty snuff box towards the "boy" who instantly sprang up and grabbed it. He showed the box to his "sister" and together they discovered how to open it. After playing with the box for some time, they showed it to the "old man." They talked for a long time.

Next morning Ostman prepared for escape. He packed his gear, shouldered his pack, injected a shell in the barrel of his rifle and started for the V-shaped opening in the rocks. The old *Sasquatch* was on guard. Ostman pointed to the opening indicating he wanted to go out. But the "old man" barred his way, pushing towards him and saying something that sounded like "Soka, Soka!" Ostman tried again but

when he received the same response, he backed up.

I didn't want to be too close if I had to shoot my way out. I only had six shells so decided to wait. There must be a better way than killing him in order to get out from here. I went back to my campsite to figure out some other way to get out.

Ostman decided to try and make friends with the young male or female. He remembered hearing about a man who saved himself from a mad bull by temporarily blinding the animal with snuff. The trick might work for Ostman if he could get close enough to the young male to put the snuff in his eyes. The next time he gave the young *Sasquatch* a snuff box, he would leave a few grains in it.

Ostman noticed that every day the young male went up the mountain to the east. He could climb as well as a mountain goat. Each time he returned with a type of grass with long roots. Ostman said the "boy" gave him some one day and it tasted very sweet. In turn, Ostman gave the young *Sasquatch* another snuff box which contained about a teaspoon of snuff. The "boy" tasted it and then took the rest to the "old man" who licked the box clean.

Later Ostman made a dipper from a milk can and a tapered stick. He demonstrated its use and then gave it to the young *Sasquatch.*

The young fellow took it to the old man and they had a long chatter. Then he came to me, pointed at the dipper then at his sister. I could see that he wanted one for her too. When I had made the dipper, I dipped it in water and drank from it, he was very pleased. Then I took a chew of snuff, smacked my lips, said, that's good.

The young fellow pointed to the old man, said something that sounded like, "Ook". I got the idea that the old man liked snuff and the young fellow wanted a box for the old man. I shook my head. I motioned with my hands for the old man to come to me. I do not think the young fellow understood what I meant.

Several days passed without much happening. Ostman felt that if he could get the "old man" to come over to him and eat a full box of snuff, "that would kill him for sure, and I wouldn't be guilty of murder".

This remark of Ostman's was very interesting. It showed clearly that, in his mind, the *Sasquatches* were above the level of animals. He observed that they were all very agile. The soles of the young male's feet were padded like a dog's and the big toe was long and very strong. To sit they turned their knees out and dropped straight down. To rise they moved straight up without help of their hands or arms.

The boy and girl were always climbing something or some other exercise. His favourite position was to take hold of his feet

Ostman felt the valley was not the family's permanent home, and that they moved from place to place as food was available. He never saw them eat meat, or do any cooking. Their food consisted mainly of grasses, roots and nuts.

Meanwhile, Ostman was running short of food. He hadn't seen any game, but had he done so he probably would not have fired his rifle. He didn't want to alarm the *Sasquatches.* The "old man" was coming closer every day.

After breakfast one morning, the "old man" and the "boy" came and sat within ten feet of Ostman. He guessed they were attracted by the aroma of the coffee. He set down the can, which was half full, and opening a new box of snuff he took "a big chew." Before he had time to close the box the "old man" reached out and grabbed it. He swallowed the entire contents and licked the box clean.

Shortly thereafter he became ill. His eyes rolled sickeningly. He grabbed the can of coffee and emptied it - grounds and all - into his mouth. That gave him no relief. He put his head between his legs and began rolling forward and squealing. Finally he jumped up and ran towards the spring.

Ostman seized this opportunity to make his escape. He quickly packed his sack and, rifle in hand, started for the opening in the wall. The young male *Sasquatch* ran to alert his mother who immediately gave chase. Ostman managed to clear the opening and then turned and fired his rifle at the rock over the "old lady's" head. Startled, she turned and ran back inside the wall. Ostman guessed it was the first time she had heard a rifle fired. He reloaded his rifle and started downhill, glancing frequently over his shoulder to ensure he was not being followed.

Sick and weak after two days in the wilderness alternately rushing on and resting, he finally stumbled into a logging camp. He asked where he was and how far it was to the nearest town.

The men said, "You look like a wild man. Where did you come from?" I told them I was a prospector and was lost. I did not like to tell them I had been kidnapped by a Sasquatch . . . they would probably have said, "He is crazy too."

The loggers helped him reach the nearest boat landing and board a steamer bound for Vancouver. That was Ostman's last prospecting trip, and his only experience with *Sasquatches.* He signed an affidavit attesting to the truth of his account of being kidnapped by a *Sasquatch* in 1924, and was cross-examined by a local magistrate, formerly a trial lawyer of considerable reputation. Afterwards the judge attested:

I cross-examined him and used every means to endeavour to find a flaw in either his personality or his story, but could find neither.

I certainly left with the impression that Mr. Ostman believes in his story himself and considers he is telling the truth. My examination and cross-examination failed to bring out any evidence to the contrary.

(signed) A. M. Naismith, Lieut-Col.

chapter four

A FACE-TO-FACE ENCOUNTER.

IN 1957, AN AGASSIZ, B.C., NEWS paper printed an interesting account by William Roe of his face-to-face meeting with a *Sasquatch.*

Roe had been keenly interested in the lives and habits of wild animals since his early boyhood when he roamed the forests of Michigan. When he became a man he moved to northern Alberta, where he supported his family by hunting and trapping. His most incredible experience with any wild creature occurred in 1955 when he was working on the highway near Tête Jaune Cache, B.C., approximately eighty miles west of Jasper, Alberta.

It was an October afternoon, and having time on his hands, Roe climbed Mica Mountain to an old deserted mine. After an easy climb, he reached the mine about three p.m. As he emerged from low brush into a clearing he saw what appeared to be the head and shoulders of a grizzly bear, about seventy-five yards away, in the brush on the other side of the open space. He decided there was no point in shooting it, because he had no way of getting it out.

He sat quietly on a rock, his rifle across his knees, and watched. A moment later the animal stood up and stepped into the clearing. Roe was astonished to see that it was not a bear. His first impression was of a huge man, about six feet tall and three feet wide, weighing approximately three hundred pounds. From head to foot the creature was covered with dark brown silver-tipped hair. As it drew nearer, Roe saw by its breasts that it was female. Its body did not curve at the waist like a female's, but was straight from shoulder to hip. Its arms were thicker than a man's, very long, and reached almost to its knees. Its feet were broader than a man's, being approximately five inches wide at the toe and tapering to sharply thinner heels. It walked by placing the heel down first, exposing the grey-brown skin on the soles of its feet.

The creature came to the edge of the brush, about twenty feet from where Roe sat. Squatting down on its haunches, it drew the branches of the bushes towards it, and stripped the leaves with its teeth.

Its lips curled flexibly around the leaves as it ate. I was close enough to see that its teeth were white and even.

The shape of this creature's head somewhat resembled a negro's. The head was higher at the back than at the front. The nose was broad and flat. The lips and chin protruded farther than its nose. But the hair that covered it, leaving bare only the parts of its face around the mouth, nose and ears, made it resemble an animal as much as a human.

Roe observed that none of the hair on its head was longer than an inch, the shortest being around the face. The creature's ears resembled a human's in shape, but its eyes were bear-like, small and black. Its neck also was unhuman, being thicker and shorter than any man's.

It occurred to Roe that a movie company might be making a film nearby, and this creature was really an actor made up to look half-animal and half-man. But he soon dismissed the idea; it would be impossible to fake such a specimen. He later confirmed there was no film company in the area at the time. According to residents of Tête Jaune Cache, no one lived up Mica Mountain.

Suddenly the creature must have sensed Roe's presence. A look of amazement crossed its face as it looked directly at the man through the bushes. Its expression was so comical that Roe could not suppress a grin. Still in crouched position, the creature took a few steps backward and then, straightening to its fullest height, hurried back across the clearing. It watched Roe briefly over its shoulder as it went, but did not seem afraid. It appeared only to desire no contact with strangers.

The thought came to me that if I shot it, I would possibly have a specimen of great interest to scientists the world over. I had heard stories about the Sasquatch, the giant hairy Indians that live in the legends of British Columbia Indians, and also many claim, are still in fact alive today. Maybe this was a Sasquatch, I told myself.

I levelled my rifle. The creature was still walking rapidly away, again turning its head to look in my direction. I lowered the rifle. Although I have called the creature "it," I felt now that it was a human being and knew I would never forgive myself if I killed it.

Reaching the brush on the other side of the clearing, the creature threw back its head and emitted a strange whinnying noise, which Roe said sounded like half-laugh and half-language. Then it disappeared into a stand of lodge-pole pine.

Roe stepped out from the brush into the clearing. As he watched, the creature reappeared on a small ridge beyond the pines, some two hundred yards away. Once again it tilted back its head and emitted the strange cry. What this cry was meant to convey Roe could not guess.

The creature disappeared then, and Roe did not see it again.

Roe was curious about the creature's habits. He wondered if it was wholly vegetarian. He looked for signs and found spoor in five different places. Upon close examination, he concluded the creature was strictly vegetarian. Further investigations showed that it had been alone, and had slept under a tree for two nights. Despite the fact the nights on the mountain were cool, there was no sign it had used a fire. There was also no indication that the creature possessed even the most primitive tools.

> . . Whether this creature was a Sasquatch I do not know. It will always remain a mystery to me, unless another one is found.
> I hereby declare the above statement to be in every part true, to the best of my powers of observation and recollection.
> (signed) William Roe,
> Sworn before William Clark, a Commissioner for Oaths in and for the Province of Alberta.

Besides the information in the sworn statement, Mr. Roe later remarked in a letter that the *Sasquatch's* fingernails were not like a bear's but were short and heavy like a man's. The animal was as deep through as it was wide, seeming almost round. There was no evidence of knotted, corded muscles as there would be in a man's arms or legs. Roe estimated that if the creature had been seven feet tall, it would have weighed something like five hundred pounds. "We have to get away from the idea of comparing it to a human being as we know them," he said.

It is interesting to note that prior to reading of William Roe's meeting with the *Sasquatch,* Albert Ostman had kept the story of his kidnapping years before to himself. Prompted by the newspaper account he contacted William Roe, related the story of his own experience and, eventually, officially recorded that story.

William Roe's face-to-face meeting with a *Sasquatch* caused such a stir in the Harrison Lake area that in 1958 the Village Council of Harrison Hot Springs sponsored a *Sasquatch* search. A reward of $5,000.00 was offered for the capture of such a creature. Vancouver newspapers printed letters protesting the hunt. Writers insisted it was wrong to bring these creatures back to civilization for exhibition purposes. They felt they should be studied scientifically and then left in peace. Nevertheless, the search took place under the leadership of twenty-six year old Rene Dahinden, a Swiss mountaineer and student of anthropology. Apart from giant footprints - some as long as seventeen inches - no *Sasquatch* was even sighted.

Over the years sightings and footprints of *Sasquatches* have become regular occurrences in British Columbia. In the fall of 1973 a track thought to be the largest ever photographed in Canada was found by Bob Uchtmann, a Manitoban Conservation Officer. It measured twenty-one inches and was one of a number of tracks he found far out in the bush.

1976 has had its quota of sightings. Earlier in the year one was reported from the Bella Coola area. *The Northern Times,* August 20th, 1976, carried another report of "giant, *Sasquatch*-like footprints" about sixteen inches long, in strides of seven feet, discovered through broken bush in the Skeena River area. The tracks were quite unlike a bear's. By their depth and length of stride, the tracks must have been made by a creature weighing eight hundred to a thousand pounds. Broken branches among the bushes indicated that the creature was considerably taller than a man. Specifics of time and place of the findings were not revealed. "The last thing we want is people bringing in a bunch of guns," said one investigator. Serious-minded researchers believe that *Sasquatch* does not live in Skeena Valley territory, but passes through the area twice yearly on its migration path.

Further excitement was aroused when it was learned a tape-recording existed of strange noises heard at night, in the general area where the footprints were found. The sounds, "somewhat akin to a cat but obviously made by a larger animal and rather more loud," were "unlike those made by any beaked creature." They are heard about twice yearly, and always set all the dogs in the neighbourhood barking furiously.

The Vancouver Sun, September 10th, 1976, gave details of another sighting. Mickey McLellan, a Kimberley fireman, and a friend, were driving about nine miles from Kimberley when they noticed a six or seven-foot tall, tan-coloured, long-armed beast in a field. "I don't know if it was a *Sasquatch* or what, but it certainly was something I'd never seen before," said Mr. McLellan. Two other cars, containing a total of six people, were also parked by the roadside watching the creature. After what seemed like three or four minutes, Mr. McLellan said, the creature "took off and started to run very fast."

A creature of the same description was seen shortly thereafter by Barbara Pretula at her store in Wycliffe, a few miles away. She managed to take a picture of the creature, before the flash in her camera scared it and it disappeared very quickly into the bush. This report appeared in *The Vancouver Sun,* and as to the authenticity of the sighting, or whether Barbara's photograph actually turned out, we shall have to rely on that newspaper.

Records now show that *Sasquatches* are known in other Canadian provinces besides British Columbia. Reports have been recorded from Yukon, Northwest Territories, Labrador, Quebec, New Brunswick, Ontario, Manitoba, Saskatchewan and Alberta.

Rene Dahinden and author-journalist John Green continue a lifetime search for the *Sasquatch.* They say the mystery is too fascinating to give up. But apart from the thousands of huge, human-like footprints found on mountain roads, creek banks and in the snow; coarse, long, dark hair found clinging to tree branches, and droppings unlike any deposited by North American game animals, we still have no tangible evidence of the *Sasquatch* in Canada.

The Americans, however, have had a little more success in this regard with their *Bigfoot.* This American equivalent of our giant wildman inhabits regions of northwestern California, Washington, Oregon, and many other states across the country. On October 20th, 1967, at Bluff Creek in northern California, a man named Roger Patterson of Yakima, Washington, captured *Bigfoot* on film. For a few seconds this huge creature, covered with glistening dark hair, looked straight into the camera, then turned and, swinging its heavy arms, crossed open ground in smooth loping strides, eventually disappearing into the forest.

From evidence given by William Roe, Albert Ostman and others, painstakingly collected and documented by experts such as John Green, Ivan Sanderson and Rene Dahinden, we have a fairly composite picture of the *Sasquatch* and his existence. Most sightings take place in summer and fall. This may be the result of man's increased outdoors activity during those seasons. The small number of winter reports could indicate that these creatures sleep through the cold weather - a conclusion reached in Russia. The *Sasquatch* is also believed to be nocturnal, since most of his activities seem to take place after dark. He is also believed to be a strong swimmer.

Footprints and John Green. Courtesy of John Green.

Indications are that *Sasquatches* lead very solitary, wandering lives, coming together only to start families and raise the young. They form individual families which remain together only until the young have become independent. The ever increasing demand for food soon breaks up a family group. Like other animals that lead similar lives, the *Sasquatch* could cover large areas in his annual wanderings.

There are still many questions whose answers will only be found on the eventual capture and subsequent study of a *Sasquatch.* If, as testimony indicates, the creature is almost entirely vegetarian, what does he eat when all vegetatian is hidden under several feet of snow? He does not appear to use tools, weapons or fire. How does he manage to keep warm in the cold winters of the northern Rockies? No bones and little organic debris have been found, but debris from other animals in the wilderness disappears very quickly and this could be the case with the *Sasquatch.* He may also bury his dead and so leave literally nothing behind him.

In recent years *Sasquatches* have been glimpsed frequently in the mountains of British Columbia, but they have never been seen near cities, parks or crowded forest recreation areas. They are not known to raid campsites for food, as do bears. They are very wary of man and, unless provoked, keep their distance.

Searches for this elusive giant have been many in recent years. Armed with tranquilizer guns, hunters have set baited traps and set out high-pitched bell-tone lures. They have strung the wilderness with electronic trip wires and have begun stalking the *Sasquatch* with high-powered rifles. Searchlights mounted on trucks probe the forest darkness for his hideaways. There is even talk of using dogs to track him down.

Man's noisy and aggressive approach only serves to alert the *Sasquatch* and drive him farther and farther into the wilderness. But man is a persistent creature, and eventually a specimen will be found and then all the fascinating and tantalizing *Sasquatch* questions will be answered.

Man will also have to look within himself for answers to other pressing questions. Is the *Sasquatch* considered man or beast? Does he have moral rights? Is it legal to cage and exhibit him? Is the killer of a *Sasquatch* a murderer?

In the meantime, I can't help feeling sorry for this monster, who, like most other creatures, only wants to live his life his own way in peace. While everybody else is busy with their questions and debates as to whether he really exists or is just an enormous "hoax," I can't help wondering - What does this mysterious, hairy giant of the wilderness think of US?

chapter five

LAKE MONSTERS: OGOPOGO

AMONG INDIAN AND ESKIMO stories there are some about serpents and monsters that live in lakes. Symbols representing these creatures were painted on birch bark, wood and rock. All through the Canadian Shield country, from Lake Mazinaw, north of Belleville, to the Ontario/Manitoba boundary, the Indian painted his stories on rock faces along the waterways. These pictographs, as they are called, told of the Indian's life at a time when mythic beasts and men lived as equals.

We can only speculate as to the true meanings of the pictographs. Perhaps the pictures merely symbolised mythical creatures, such as *Mishipizhiw,* the Ojibway demigod of water. Perhaps the Indians really believed monstrous serpents lived in the waters. The accompanying chart shows some Indian pictograph sites where symbols of serpents and monsters are depicted.   (Taken and compiled from: *Indian Rock Paintings of the Great Lakes* by Selwyn Dewdney and Kenneth E. Kidd, University of Toronto Press.)

Canada is dotted with a myriad lakes, some very deep and remote, where monsters could live virtually unnoticed and undisturbed. LAKE OKANAGAN, British Columbia, on the Pacific slopes of the Rockies, is such a lake. In geological time this lake is young, only recently having been cut off from the sea. Sixty-nine miles long and varying in width from three quarters to two-and-a-half miles, the lake has an area of about one hundred and twenty miles. Twenty-two miles up from Penticton, at a bend in the lake, there is a small, barren and rocky island. Over one hundred years ago the local Indians regarded the

PICTOGRAPH SITES WHERE SYMBOLS OF MONSTERS ARE DEPICTED.

Site.	Description.
NAMAKAN NARROWS (the east end of Rainy Lake - Quetico-Superior country).	Serpent.
SABASKONG BAY	
OBABIKON BAY (Lake of the Woods South of Aulneau Peninsula).	A serpent 15 feet long, with open mouth, ears and three large flippers (strikingly similar to Ogopogo, discussed later in this chapter).
	2 smaller serpentine figures (one with antlers, the other with horns, symmetrically facing a large turtle).
SIOUX NARROWS.	Serpent monster, jaws and foreflippers.
DRYBERRY LAKE (North end of the lake).	Serpentine form (seen in various versions in other places).
PICTURED LAKE (from Oliver Lake, 20 miles south-west of Fort William).	Serpent: eyes in a triangular head.
AGAWA BAY (Lake Superior Provincial Park).	A great serpent and two smaller ones. The great serpent is believed to be MI-SHI-PI-ZHIW (Great Lynx), sinister deity of swift or troubled waters, who is still feared and revered west and north of the Sault.
ABAMATAGWIA and BASKET LAKES (Locally known as "Fishtrap").	Serpentine form.
LES PETITS ECRIT (Little Cove) - Lake Superior).	Monsters: snakes with wings.
LAKE TIMAGAMI	Snake-like form.
GEORGIAN BAY (shore - west of French River).	Huge snake-like form.

water surrounding the island with superstition. There, they said, in the forbidding depths lived *Naitaka,* the monster spirit of the lake. Always when venturing out on the lake the Indians stayed well away from the island and carried a chicken or a pup which they dropped into the murky water to appease the monster spirit.

They tell an interesting story about a visiting chief named Timbasket,

Ogopogo. Courtesy of the Provincial Archives, Victoria, B.C.

who chose to disregard the practice of appeasing the monster. Despite warnings against incurring *Naitaka's* anger, he set out with his family in a canoe to cross the lake. Halfway across there was a sudden upheaval in the water under his canoe and he and his family were swallowed up by the swirling foam and never seen again.

The Indians' superstitious dread of the monster spirit, or *Soore-Appos* (Water-Demon), continued even after the white man began settling in the Okanagan Valley. Stories passed on to the settlers recalled how often in the past the beaches of Monster's Island had been littered with the bloody remains of *Naitaka's* meals.

In 1854 a Métis told how a team of horses he was swimming across the lake behind his canoe were suddenly pulled down into the water by some strong force. He had to cut them loose for fear of being drowned himself. Wary of the Indian stories, and having seen a strange animal in the lake themselves, the settlers continued the custom of "appeasing the monster" with small offerings.

One of the early pioneers of the Okanagan Valley, Mrs. Allison, who died in 1928, made an extensive study of Indian folklore, and contributed many articles on the subject to journals. She herself was not superstitious. One day, when her husband was across the lake getting supplies at Okanagan Mission, a sudden storm blew up. Worried for his safety, Mrs. Allison went out on the cliffs overlooking the lake near their cabin to watch for his return. There was no sign of his boat but across the rainswept water she saw something that looked like a log. As she watched, it began to move with a slight undulating motion against the waves.

A few moments later it disappeared. When her husband finally returned safely she told him her story. He only laughed. But he remembered his wife's words later on, when he heard of another incident. It concerned a friend, John McDougall, and was similar to the experience of the Métis in 1854. Mr. McDougall was also bringing a team of horses across the lake behind his boat. Although he believed, like the Indians, in appeasing the monster, he apparently forgot to bring an offering. In the middle of the lake his horses were suddenly pulled down. Fearing his boat would be overturned and he drowned with his horses, he cut them loose.

The settlers' name for the monster was *Ogopogo,* and the name has stuck. Believers continue to affirm his existence, but whereas the Indians left crude drawings of *Naitaka* on stone, the citizens of Kelowna have immortalized *Ogopogo* with a statue.

Ogopogo has been seen repeatedly since the beginning of this century. Descriptions vary. Sometimes only a black hump - or a series of humps - is observed moving swiftly in the lake; at other times a head and neck are seen.

On July 2, 1949, a Mr. Kray and a family named Watson from Montreal were cruising off Kelowna when they saw a dark shape drifting north. Mr. Kray described what the party witnessed:

> *. . . a long sinuous body, 30 feet in length, consisting of about 5 undulations, apparently separated from each other by about a 2 foot space, in which that part of the undulations would have been underwater. The length of each of the undulations that could be seen would have been about 5 feet. There appeared to be a forked tail, of which only one-half came above the water. From time to time the whole thing submerged and came up again.*

The tail described by Mr. Kray has seldom been mentioned by other witnesses, probably because it is not so much a tail as a bilobated pair of flippers.

The monster finally moved away, apparently in pursuit of a shoal of fish, leaving a great wake. When the party first saw the monster it was swimming in about six feet of water and appeared to be feeding on weeds that grow to the surface near the shore.

On a Sunday morning in July, 1952, Mrs. E. W. Campbell of Vancouver was visiting her sister-in-law, Mrs. E. A. Campbell, at her Kelowna home. As they sat on the lawn looking across the lake the monster suddenly appeared a few hundred feet off shore:

> *I am a stranger here. I did not even know such things existed. But I saw it so plainly. A head like a cow or horse that reared right out of the water. It was a wonderful sight. The coils glistened like two huge wheels . . . There were ragged edges like a saw (along its back). It was so beautiful with the sun shining on it. It was all so clear, so extraordinary. It came up three times, then submerged and disappeared.*

Another sighting, by Reverend W. S. Beams, rector of St. Saviours Anglican Church, Penticton, B.C., was reported in *The Penticton Herald* on Saturday, 12th August, 1950:

> *The day was bright, sunny and the lake was calm. Suddenly there was a terrific disturbance in the water and several humps appeared. "It was like a huge hose threshing about in the water." After some three or four minutes the "animal" disappeared below the surface, leaving a terrific wake behind.*

More recent sightings have been reported in *The Kelowna Courier:*

> *17th July, 1963 - 72 year old Sy Jenkins was fishing in the bay at Naramanta Bay, when he noticed a commotion in an overgrown section of the lake. A 20 foot long black object, showing 3 humps about 5 feet apart, travelled past the boat and moved into deep water. Mr. Jenkins said the serpent was visible for more than a minute. A Naramanta resident for a number of years, he has never before seen the Ogopogo though he has fished in the*

lake a great deal.

Summer of 1964 - A Mr. and Mrs. Leslie Kerry saw something about 300 yards off shore, creating a large wave. It moved about a mile down the lake, watched carefully through binoculars. Mr. Kerry said: "I could distinctly see a head and part of a shoulder. It looked very much like a seal head, although I thought I could make out two horns. It was travelling very fast and making quite a commotion . . . "

September 3, 1964 - Kenny Unser, aged 15, throwing sticks into the water for his dog, near the Kelowna old Ferry wharf noticed high waves, and then about three feet of dark-green tail came out of the water and hit the wharf with a crash . . . "It was about 75 yards away . . . about a foot thick, with big scales, and rounded off at the end like a chopped-off dog's tail . . . it hit hard, and water splashed up onto the wharf."

Frightened, Kenny got his dog out of the water and went home. His family treated his story as a joke until they learned two other people had reported seeing something large moving in the water a few hours previously, near the Ogopogo statue; close to the old Ferry Wharf. Mrs. Dorothy Parrish and Mrs. Betty Nordvie noticed something 100 yards out and wondered if it could be a submarine, "but I realised it was too shallow." They could see "the water moving over what appeared to be three humps . . ." There were no boats in the area at the time.

Sightings of *Ogopogo's* frightening, undulating body with its shiny scales and whipping tail have continued through the years. But they always occur in the warm summer months. No one ever sees him between October and May. It is believed he hibernates during the winter months in a cave somewhere beneath Monster's Island.

The Globe and Mail of July 9th, 1976, reported *Ogopogo's* first appearance of the year. On Tuesday, July 6th, two fishermen, Stan Barron of Calgary and Lawney Scown of Coral Beach, were fishing near Fintry on the west side of the lake, when the monster appeared.

> *We were approximately 300 yards off shore,* (Mr. Baron said). *It* (the monster) *was swimming parallel to shore about 100 yards further out in the lake. The creature was attempting to push us toward the shore . . . It was blue-black. We saw the head and tail appear as it moved in a caterpillar-like fashion in the water.*

The men were concerned about the heavy wake behind the monster and feared getting too close. Mr. Baron said they got the distinct impression that they were "crowding the creature's territory and that it was upset." He gave the monster's length as approximately forty to sixty feet. The two men watched it for five minutes. As they crossed the lake on their return trip to Coral Beach, they saw it again.

I thought Ogopogo was a myth (continued Mr. Baron). *I'm convinced there was a creature in the lake. I'd like to have another look at him — this time with a camera.*

According to *The Globe and Mail,* as of July 31st, there had been five separate sightings of *Ogopogo* in 1976. While his formidable appearance still strikes fear into the hearts of many, Canadians in general have come to regard *Ogopogo* with affection, much as the Britons do their "Nessie." Indeed, in recent years descriptions of him do seem to have become less frightening.

There have been some fuzzy photographs taken of *Ogopogo,* and many theories formulated as to his really being an optical illusion caused by the play of the sun on the waves. But monster-loving Okanagan's who have witnessed his appearances steadfastly insist he *is* a *real, live monster.*

In addition to being the subject of a sculpture in Kelowna's lakeside park, *Ogopogo* has been commemorated in other ways. There is a stadium at the Aquatic Centre named after him; likewise, an annual golf tournament held near the city. His name is associated with many commercial business and tourist enterprises and in return *Ogopogo* obligingly manages to put in an appearance each year just before Kelowna's annual regatta in August. There was even a song written about him in 1924. It was sung by Bill Primblecome at a dinner in Vernon, near the northern end of the Lake Okanagan system, for Vancouver Board of Trade visitors. The words went something like this:

His mother was an earwig,
His father was a whale,
A little bit of head
And hardly any tail —
And Ogopogo *was his name . . .*

No doubt in time Lake Okanagan's deep and mysterious waters will be subjected to intense scientific probing, and then, at last, *Ogopogo* and all his ancient history will be revealed.

chapter six

LAKE MONSTERS: MANIPOGO and IGOPOGO.

LAKE MANITOBA IS JUST THE kind of place where you would expect to find a monster. The landscape surrounding the one hundred and twenty-four square miles of water is tree-lined and lonely and reminiscent of Scandinavia. Icelandic settlers were attracted to the lake in the nineteenth century for just this reason. Like the *Skrimsl,* Scandinavia's answer to the *Loch Ness Monster,* a Canadian monster soon became part of their folklore. *Manipogo* is its name, and it is a resident of Lake Manitoba, Lake Winnipegosis, and Dauphin Lake.

Probably the earliest recorded sighting was that of a Hudson's Bay Company fur trader named Valentine McKay, in 1909, although there was some mention of this monster having been seen the year before. According to Mr. McKay, he saw a "huge creature travelling at a speed of about two miles an hour. It had a dark upper surface which glistened, and part of the body projected about four feet in the air, vertically. The water was considerably disturbed." The monster disappeared behind an island.

Rumors about this monster, and his responsibility for the sudden upheaval of ice on the lake in midwinter, persisted until 1935 when a timber inspector named C. F. Ross and Tom Spence saw a strange animal at the north end of Lake Winnipegosis. It had a small, flat head, from the back of which a single horn protruded "like a periscope." The body was dull grey in colour and resembled a dinosaur.

In 1948 there was another report from Lake Manitoba. Near St. Rose du Lac, C.P. Alric suddenly heard an unearthly cry. Then, in the marshes about four hundred yards away, a "brownish-black thing about six feet long" rose up for a moment.

In August of 1955, near Graves Point - and as a point of interest, in the same place where trapper McKay saw his monster in 1909 - Joe Parker, Albert Gott and two of his sons saw something "rise about four feet out of the water." It was about two-and-a-half feet thick. They were able to row within four hundred yards of it before it disappeared.

A month later, near Overflowing River on Lake Winnipegosis, Charles Burrell and three Americans saw four to six feet of an animal's back break the surface of the lake.

In 1957 a serpent-like animal was seen on Lake Manitoba by Louis Betcher and Edie Napanik who were working on the shore. This report and others that same year - one of which told of hearing "a bellow like a goods train whistle" - aroused such concern among the residents that the local government sent a team to search the lake. "The safety and prosperity of many Manitobans are tied up with this expedition and we hope it will prosper," said Mr. Jobin, the State Minister of Industry and Commerce. The search failed to reveal the monster and the team returned. Reports continued to come in.

Three years later, in July, 1960, Mr. A. R. Adams of St. Rose saw "a creature resembling a large snake, with a diamond shaped head eight inches wide" swimming at approximately fifteen miles per hour. There was a wake about eight feet wide and fifteen inches high behind the head. Sometime later, and fourteen miles away, Mr. Christopher Stople, his wife and her sister saw "a reptile-like beast" surface some thirty feet away from their boat. The women were so frightened they left the boat and waded ashore through a marsh.

A large "reptile" was seen by twenty people at Manipogo Beach on July 22nd and three weeks later, August 12th, three monsters - two large and a small - were seen on the same beach by seventeen people.

Dr. James A. MacLeod, Chairman of the Zoology Department of the University of Manitoba, who had followed the recovery of the coelacanth off the South African coast in 1938 with great interest, theorized that primitive animals long considered extinct could still exist in places like Lake Manitoba and Loch Ness, Scotland. He organized an expedition which he led to the northern end of Lake Manitoba in search of the animal. The search was not successful and the monster remained as much a mystery as before. Dr. MacLeod did not give up, however. He announced that he would search the lake again the following year early in August, 1961, but this time he would engage skilled help and equipment. Skin divers would search the lake bottom for remains of the monster.

At approximately 8:30 p.m. on Saturday, August 19th, 1961, a group of seven people were watching the lake from Twin Beaches. "Isn't that a boat sinking?" Mrs. Blanche Konecki asked. "No," came the reply from another of the group. "It's the monster!" They watched the monster for four or five minutes. Mr. Patrick Rakowski described it as follows: "It was over forty feet long with one large hump - about thirty-five feet long - and a short hump at the end. It was yellowy-brown and looked slimey." They estimated the monster's swimming speed was five to seven miles per hour.

By now the newspapers had given the monster a name - *Manipogo* - after the monster in Lake Okanagan. The following year - 1962 - and again in early August, fishermen reported seeing *Manipogo*. On August

12th two fishermen, Richard Vincent and John Konafell, assisted by an American television commentator, managed to photograph the monster. Mr. Vincent reported:

> We first spotted the object to the left of our boat about 300 yards away. After swinging into the direction it was heading we saw what we believed to be a large black snake or eel - . . . which was swimming with ripple action . . . It was about a foot in girth and about 12 feet of the monster was above water. No head was visible.

The hump in the photograph was estimated to be two feet high. Since the gunwale of the fishermen's boat appears in the photograph, their estimate that the monster was fifty to seventy-five yards away would be fairly accurate. Though their boat had a ten horsepower outboard motor the monster quickly outdistanced them.

In Dr. MacLeod's opinion the photograph was genuine. "If that isn't the monster, I'd like to know what the deuce it is," he said.

There is yet a third in the 'Pogo group of monsters. Igopogo is the name given to a creature in Lake Simcoe, forty miles from Toronto. Like other Canadian monsters, Igopogo first had his place in Indian legend. There were persistent reports of sightings among settlers during the nineteenth century and on and off thereafter, but none were taken very seriously until 1952 when the monster was reported seen by an Indian trapper.

The Oakville Journal Record carried another report on July 27th, 1963, of a sighting at Keswick, Ontario:

> A Presbyterian minister, a funeral director and their families are the latest to claim to have seen Igopogo, the Lake Simcoe sea-serpent. The Rev. L. B. Williams of Mount Albert and Neil Lathangue of Bradford, their wives and children were boating in the lake on Monday when something came towards them. Mr. Lathangue said it was charcoal coloured, 30 to 70 feet long and had dorsal fins.

Another witness was quoted as saying the monster was a "dog-faced animal with a neck the diameter of a stove-pipe."

chapter seven

OTHER LAKE MONSTERS!

THE FIRST REPORT OF THE LAKE

Utopia Monster was given over one hundred years ago by a man named Leith Adams. Lumbermen working at a sawmill at one end of the usually calm lake in Charlotte County, N.B., suddenly noticed a huge splashing object in the water. Several of the witnesses stated it was at least ten feet wide and thirty feet long. Similar reports came in over the next two days from different parts of the lake.

The Illustrated News of Canada published the first report. The monster, it stated, was raising "Old Ned" and "was sending up logs, spruce edgings and other material and causing the water to boil and foam as if a geyser had suddenly broken loose."

A few years ago, on the eighteenth anniversary of the last reported sighting of this famous monster, newspapers in St. John, N.B., featured an interview with an eyewitness. Although almost ninety years old, Mrs. Fred McKillop could still recall the incident quite clearly:

> It is still fresh in my mind, and I was never so frightened in my life.
> It was a beautiful day. The men had all gone fishing and had left me to sit with two of my grandchildren. We were all watching the lake and it was beautiful. It was so clear it resembled glass and there wasn't a ripple showing.

It is interesting to note that, in the case of marine monsters in general, sightings seem to occur only when the water is smooth and calm.

Suddenly, as I watched the water commenced to boil and churn and make waves which came in and broke on the shore. Then a huge creature of some sort emerged from the water, at least it showed part of its head and part of its body. It resembled a huge black rock, but it moved and churned all the time. I was alone with the grandchildren at our cabin, and was so terrified that I took the children and ran into the cabin and locked the door.

After a short time had passed, I realised that whatever it was belonged in the lake and so we were in no danger. It was then I went outside again and watched it.

It moved back and forth across the lake, boiling and churning the water, and making waves. I don't recall exactly how long I watched, but it seemed to be a long time.

I had never before heard of the Lake Utopia Monster, *and therefore, had no idea what it was. When the men returned home I told them about it and they said that must have been what it was. I recall it as a very frightening experience.*

Numerous reports by people who claim to have seen the *Lake Utopia Monster* are contained in the Ganong Collection at the New Brunswick Museum. Sightings usually occur after the winter ice breaks up on the lake. Visitors are drawn to the lake at this time of the year, especially in the hopes of seeing the ugly head breaking through the ice and opening up the lake for the start of the season.

MOCKING LAKE, Quebec.

Reports of a monster in Mocking Lake, Quebec, reach back for almost one hundred years, and have been seriously investigated. In 1958 the Director of the Quebec Department of Game and Fisheries, Dr. Vadim Vladikov, went out to the lake to conduct a personal investigation:

I have questioned a great many people in Saint Eleuthre and they tell me the same thing . . . an animal between 12 and 18 feet long, brown or black in colour, with a round back 2 or 3 feet wide and a sawtooth fin down the centre. Any time anyone approaches close, the animal slithers away and sinks below the lake's surface.

LAKE POHENEGAMOOK, Quebec.

A monster is purported to live in Lake Pohenegamook, two hundred and eighty miles northeast of Montreal, near the New Brunswick border. An article in *The Hamilton Spectator* on October 6th, 1976, described it as "a thing from another time, black and dragon-like, as long as three canoes, fast as a motor boat, yet quiet as a midnight breeze."

Abbe Leopold Plante, a seventy-four year old retired priest, told of seeing the monster some twenty years ago, when sightings were an everyday occurrence. Although the abbe's experience occurred so long ago, the memory still "burns" in his mind. His description of the creature somewhat resembles a giant iguana; scaly and black, with a head like a cow's.

> The lake was as calm as a mirror. You could see a toothpick floating.
> All of a sudden, about 1,000 feet from shore I saw this black thing floating. It was like two pieces with a depression in the middle. Then, as I was pulling in my line (fishing), it went shwoosh and it was gone.

In 1957 Dr. Vadim Vladikov wanted to place a powerful net across the mile-wide lake to catch the monster, but he was unable to raise the necessary three thousand dollars and so the venture was abandoned.

In the past, newspapers have carried stories of people fearing to go boating or swimming in the lake because of the creature, but over the years, the citizens of Pohenegamook have developed a more neighbourly attitude towards their monster. He was the town mascot during its 1974 centennial celebrations when his likeness, drawn by a local artist, graced the official ceremonial handbook.

LAKE DUCHENE, Ontario/Quebec.

The Toronto Globe of July 8th, 1880, reported a strange occurrence the year before on Lake Duchene, an enlargement of the Ottawa River. A French Canadian fisherman was startled one night on the lake when a dark object suddenly rushed past him. The strange object was also seen on July 6th, 1880, by two men on the north shore of the lake near a phosphate mine.

> Mr. Williams, the foreman of the mine and a French Canadian named Blanchette, noticed the water of the lake was agitated about one-eighth of a mile out, between Little Island lighthouse and the shore. After watching a moment, the French Canadian cried out, "Le Serpent!" Mr. Williams says that the creature in the water was a serpent of some kind and a very large one at that. It wriggled along in the water quite fast. They could see about 4 feet of its back from the head, but it appeared to be more than three times that length from the motion of the water, while in thickness its body seemed to be about the size of a small telegraph pole. It was a dark green in colour.

The men rushed back to the mine for guns, but when they returned the monster had disappeared, leaving only ripples on the surface. A farmer named Mr. Bradley and his sons had seen the creature at the same place once before.

MUSKRAT LAKE.
Hapyxelor is the name the people of Cobden, sixty miles northwest of Ottawa, have given to a monster believed to live in Muskrat Lake.

Ten miles long and in some places as deep as two hundred and forty feet, the lake has long been the scene of local legend.

"Mussy" — as the monster is affectionately called — is silver-green in colour, has three eyes, three ears, one big fin halfway down his back, two legs and one big tooth in front. He is twenty-four feet long, eats fish and is considered friendly.

A recent sighting of Hapyxelor was reported in *The Ottawa Citizen*. About 8.30 p.m. on June 7th, 1976, sixteen year old Allan Childerhose and his seventeen year old friend John Hoad were on the shore of Muskrat Lake when their attention was attracted by a splashing sound. An object was moving through the water about half a mile from shore, causing ripples and the sound.

> *Trailing about thirty feet behind and cutting the surface was a "green fin of some sort."*
>
> *The two boys watched for about five minutes while it continued to move down the lake towards Cobden, on the opposite shore. The fin dipped up and down in the water . . .*
>
> *The fin moved down the lake about 400 yards and then, said Allan, sank out of sight near the outer limits of Cobden. The boy said it could not have been a scuba diver because of its shape and size.*

Allan Childerhose said the sight had left him unnerved. "I felt a little weird . . . I didn't know what to make of it . . ." The boys talked immediately to several people who were camping nearby. They had seen a "strange wave" and "something moving in the water."

Frank and Betty Stark also saw something in the water which Mr. Stark described as "two bumps with a space in between them." He said it was moving in a southeasterly direction, but had no discernible colour. The object was visible for two or three minutes and then "it just disappeared."

Over the years there have been reports of various phenomena in the lake; included among them are detailed descriptions of "a large aquatic animal."

LAKE ERIE.

While in Canada's early days people did not attach too much importance to stories of monsters in the lakes, in other countries they were taken more seriously. In 1819, an article on sea snakes appeared in France, written by the brilliant scientist Samuel Rafinesque, which mentioned a monster seen in Lake Erie in July, 1817. There were two reports of this monster, one stating it was thirty-five feet long, one foot round and dark mahogany coloured, and the other giving it bright eyes and a length nearer sixty feet. Rafinesque thought it might have been a giant eel.

LAKE ONTARIO.

A German science journal published an account of a monster seen in Lake Ontario in 1835, but the facts about this monster are not readily attainable.

OTHER LAKE MONSTERS.

The Cree Indians claim there lives a fish-like serpent in Lake Meminisha, on the Albany River in Ontario. A monster the Indians call *Ta-Zum-A* lives in Lake Sushwap, B.C.; another called *Tsinquaw,* lives in Cowichan Lake on Vancouver Island; and still others live in Lake Champlain, Quebec, and Lake Iliamna, Alaska.

The Indians, who for so long had Canada to themselves, roaming the lands, forests and lakes at will, told about many more lake monsters. For the most part these stories were dismissed by the white man as mere legends. Yet it is conceivable that monsters could exist wherever the water is deep and quiet. Some scientists and monster experts believe these huge lake monsters formerly lived in the seas. The lakes of Canada were once fjords until the land level rose sometime between the end of the last Ice Age (more than ten thousand years ago) and five thousand years ago. Trapped in lakes, the (sea) monsters probably survived because the food and conditions were right.

Sightings of lake monsters go on, although they are less frequent than they used to be. Canadians are very keen boaters and water-skiers and often the smallest of lakes will be alive with noise and activity at weekends and throughout the summer months. At such times monsters must prefer to give man and his noisy pastimes a wide berth!

chapter eight

SEA-SERPENTS - EAST COAST.

IT HAS BEEN SAID THAT THERE IS is probably no more fascinating creature in the minds of men than the elusive sea-serpent. Men have been describing it since the beginnings of civilization.

The sea-serpent, a creature resembling a giant snake with a neck rising from a slim body with flippers, was often depicted in stories and pictures in Medieval times and much earlier.

In the twelfth century the Persian cosmographer Kazvini wrote about the "fish shaped like a camel." (As it happens, one type of sea-serpent is very much like a camel in head shape and humps.)

Early sailors believed a great Midguard Serpent called *Jormungard* encircled the world at the equator at the bottom of the sea, with its tail in its mouth. This belief continued even to the sixteenth century, after sailors learned the world was round.

Though man's belief in other mythical creatures waned long ago, his belief in the great sea-serpent has persisted even to modern times. Eminent scientists, such as Samuel Rafinesque-Smaltz, Anton Cornelius Oudemans, Ivan Sanderson and Bernard Heuvelmans, have researched and written extensively on the subject. As a result we have quite a composite picture of the sea-serpent, its variations, and its territories.

Sea-serpents can be divided into the following categories:

1. *Long-necked.*
2. *Merhorse.*
3. *Many-humped.*
4. *Super-eel.*
5. *Super-otter.*
6. *Marine Saurians.*
7. *Many-finned.*
8. *Yellow-Belly.*

Of these the first four appear in Canadian waters.

The Long-necked: *Polar regions, North Atlantic* off Newfoundland, East of the *North Pacific* off *British Columbia.*

A fairly large sized animal, long slender neck, small round head, tapering muzzle.
Eyes very small. Two little horns sometimes seen on head.

A great migrator, is known for its remarkably high cruising speed. *Frequently met on the high seas.*

By far the most sightings. Considered to be *a "rising species."*

Merhorse: *Polar seas, North Atlantic,* near *Nova Scotia, North Pacific* near *British Columbia* and *Southeast Alaska.*

Long slender body, very large. Long neck with floating mane. Head tapering in profile - like a horse's or camel's; diamond-shaped from front. Enormous eyes. Very wide mouth and thick lips. Whiskers on face. The back sometimes has a jagged crest.

Moves with marked vertical undulations. Is capable of considerable speed.

Cosmopolitan. Territory on West Coast *north* to *Juneau, Alaska* and as far *south* as *Los Angeles.*

Sighted all year round. Nocturnal habits. *"Rising species."*

Many-humped: *North Atlantic,* between *Newfoundland and New York.* Warm water of Gulf Stream.

Sea animal of great size, elongated body with a number of fins - often shows four to twelve triangular fins above the water. Round head like a seal or calf. Small prominent eyes, high on head. Very wide mouth, like a turtle's. Hairs on front of muzzle around nostrils. Short slender neck.

Moves in vertical undulations. Can reach ten knots, when chased.

Becoming much rarer.

Super-eels: *Atlantic, Nova Scotia.*

Usually not over fifty feet in length. Long neck, cylindrical body. Long tail tapering to a point.

The only sea-serpents truly serpentine.

Some have a blunt head like a common eel; others, pointed like a moray or conger. Eyes, very large. Some pectoral fins.

Cosmopolitan and abyssal.

Sea-serpents seem to be a cosmopolitan breed. They share a marked taste for fine weather, being rarely seen except in warm, sunny weather and calm seas. They prefer to swim in warm ocean currents, spending the summer months in the Northern Hemisphere and migrating in the winter to the Southern Hemisphere.

A great number of sea-serpent sightings have been recorded; numbered among witnesses are such personages as scientists, priests and bishops.

In an article he wrote in 1817, the French-American scientist Rafinesque-Schmaltz wrote of a two hundred foot long sea-serpent seen by Mrs. W. Lee, in 1805, near Cape Breton and Newfoundland. She stated: "Its back was dark green and it stood in the water in flexuous hillocks and went through it with impetuous noise."

The first recorded sighting in Canadian waters was on July 15th, 1825, in Halifax Harbour. It was seen by several people from entirely separate positions. They described it as having "a body as big as a tree trunk . . . The animal had about eight coils or humps to its body and it was about sixty feet long."

A similar creature was seen the next summer by William Warburton, south of Newfoundland.

On May 15th, 1833, in Mahone Bay, forty miles west of Halifax, three officers and two enlisted men of Her Majesty's Navy were relaxing on the deck of a fishing boat when they sighted at a distance of one hundred and fifty to two hundred yards:

> . . . the head and neck of some denizen of the deep, precisely like those of a common snake, in the act of swimming, the head so far elevated and thrown forward by the curve of the neck as to enable us to see the water under and beyond it. The creature rapidly passed, leaving a regular wake, from the commencement of which, to the forepart, which was out of water, we judged its length to be about 80 feet; and this within rather than beyond the mark . . .
>
> It is most difficult to give correctly the dimensions of any object in the water. The head of the creature we set down at about six feet in length, and the portion of the neck which we saw, at the same; the extreme length, as before stated, at between 80 and 100 feet. The neck in thickness equalled the bole of a moderate-sized tree. The head and neck of a dark brown or nearly black colour, streaked with white in irregular streaks.

The five principal witnesses signed with their names, ranks, and dates on which they received their commissions:

W. SULLIVAN, Captain, Rifle Brigade, June 21, 1831.

A. MACLACHLAN, Lieutenant, ditto, August 5, 1824.

C. P. MALCOLM, Ensign, ditto, August 13, 1830.

B. O'NEAL LYSTER, Lieut. Artillery, June 7, 1816.

HENRY INCE, Ordnance Storekeeper at Halifax.

In his book *A Second Visit to the United States of North America* Sir Charles Lyell tells of a marine monster which appeared at Merigomish on the northern coast of Nova Scotia. The information was gathered for him by geologist J. W. Dawson, with whom Lyell had previously explored Nova Scotia, in 1842.

The monster was reported to be "about one hundred feet long, and was nearly aground in calm water, within two hundred feet of the beach. It remained in sight about half an hour, and then got off with difficulty."

One of the witnesses went up a bank in order to look down upon it. They said it sometimes raised its head (which resembled that of a seal) partially out of the water. Along its back were a number of humps or protuberances, which, in the opinion of the observer on the beach, were true humps, while the other thought they were produced by vertical flexures of the body. Between the head and the first protuberance there was a straight part of the back of considerable length, and this part was generally above water. The colour appeared black, and the skin had a rough appearance.

The animal was seen to bend its body almost into a circle, and again to unbend it with rapidity. It was slender in proportion to its length. After it had disappeared in deep water, its wake was visible for some time. There were no indications of paddles seen. Some other persons who saw it, compared the creature to a long string of fishing-net buoys moving rapidly about.

In the course of the summer, the fishermen on the eastern shore of Prince Edward's Island, in the Gulf of St. Lawrence, had been terrified by this sea monster, and the year before, October, 1844, a similar creature swam slowly past the pier at Arisaig, near the east end of Nova Scotia, and, there being only a slight breeze at the time, was attentively observed by Mr. Barry, a millwright of Pictou, who told Mr. Dawson he was within 120 feet of it, and estimated its length at 60 feet, and the thickness of its body at three feet. It had humps on the back, which seemed too small and close together to be bends of the body.

The body appeared also to move in long undulations, *including many of the smaller humps. In consequence of this motion, the head and tail were sometimes both out of sight, and sometimes both above water, as represented in the annexed outline, given from memory.*

The head . . . was rounded and obtuse in front, and was never elevated more than a foot above the surface. The tail was pointed, appearing like half of a mackerel's tail. The colour of the part seen was black.

Mysterious carcass on beach at Framboise, N.S., in July, 1976, identified as basking shark. Photo-Owen Fitzgerald

It was suggested to Mr. Dawson that a swell in the sea might give the deceptive appearance of an undulating movement, as it is well known "that a stick held horizontally at the surface of water when there is a ripple seems to have an uneven outline." But Mr. Barry replied that he observed the animal very attentively, having read accounts of the sea-serpent, and feels confident that the undulations were not those of the water.

In the summer of 1849, Joseph Holland, Jacob Kedy and two other fishermen saw something large and long swimming near the shore on South West Island on the west of the entrance to St. Margaret's Bay, Nova Scotia. They launched a boat and upon investigation discovered what looked like a snake some sixty feet long. Here is their story as reported by Rev. John Ambrose:

It was proportioned like an eel, i.e. tapering towards the extremities with no caudel fin perceptible, but one very high fin, or row of spines, each of about an inch in diameter at the base, erected along its back serving indeed for a dorsal fin, like the folding fin of the Thymnus vulgaris, or albicore. This spinal erection seemed to occupy about one third of its length, each end of it being about equi-distant from the Serpent's extremities; and at a distance, somewhat resembling, in size and appearance, the sail of a skiff. The animal's back was covered with scales, about six inches long and three inches wide, extending in rows across the body, i.e., the longer diameter of the scale being in the direction of the circumference of the body. The colour of the back was black. The men had no opportunity of seeing the belly, but what the American would call 'a smart chance' of becoming acquainted with the inside of it; for the creature, perceiving the boat, raised its head about ten feet above water, turned towards it, and opened its jaws, showed the inside of its mouth red in colour and well armed with teeth about three inches long, shaped like those of a cat-fish. The men now thinking it high time to terminate the interview, pulled vigorously for shore, followed for some distance by the snake, which at length gave up the chase and disappeared.

Although this description is very detailed, something about it does not quite ring true. Dr. Bernard Heuvelmans, author/zoologist ("The Sherlock Holmes of zoology" as he is known in France), felt that if the description "is truthful and accurate, it seems more to apply to a reptile, which can move its head on its neck. But as such an animal . . . has never been described by anybody else, even in a work of palaentology, this report is unacceptable and seems very suspect."

There are dozens of reports such as this one, wherein something does not quite fit the usual pattern of sea-serpents, formed by experts such as Dr. Heuvelmans after painstaking documentation and cross-reference of hundreds of reports. I shall henceforth relate only those descriptions which have passed the eagle eyes of the experts!

We move on to the 30th August, 1913, to an interesting and colourful description of an encounter by the Allan Line steamer *Corinthian,* with a "Sea-giraffe" on the Grand Bank of Newfoundland. The animal was seen by the quartermaster, Ayres, and by the second officer, G. Batchelor, who gave the following account:

> As the Corinthian *was ploughing her way westward I was officer of the watch 'on duty at the time'. At 4.30 a.m. in the cold gray dawn of August 30th, 1913, on The Grand Banks of Newfoundland, the lookout man had just gone off and the third officer had left the Bridge . . . while casting my eyes around the horizon I picked up an object about a mile off right ahead. The best conjecture I could make as to its nature was that it was a fishing boat laying end on to us. In the dense and extensive fogs which sweep over the fishing banks sailors frequently become separated from their schooners and many starve for days before they are picked up. I had such an accident in mind as I watched the object ahead. When it suddenly disappeared beneath the surface, being still unenlightened I thought of tragedy. Suddenly . . . something surprising showed itself about two hundred feet away from the ship.*
>
> *First appeared a great head, long fin-like ears and great blue eyes. The eyes were mild and liquid, with no indication of ferocity.*
>
> *Following sad eyes came a neck, it was a regular neck all right, all of twenty feet in length which greatly resembled a giraffe.*
>
> *The monster took its time in emerging, but it kept emerging so long that I wondered what the end would be.*
>
> *The neck . . . seemed to be set on a ball-bearing, so supple was it and so easily and rhythmically did it sway while the large liquid blue eyes took in the ship with a surprised, injured and fearful stare. The creature was well fixed for side arms. Three horned fins surmounted its bony head, probably for defence and attack or for ripping things up. The body was about the same length as the neck very much like that of a monster seal or sea-lion with short water-smoothed fur.*
>
> *The tail was split into two large fins.*
>
> *Its colour scheme was good, although some might think it giddy; light brownish-yellow tastefully spattered with spots of a darker hue.*
>
> *For a minute the creature inspected the Corinthian with its roving gaze, and then it disappeared, showing its after-works as it dived. Its whole attitude while in sight was that of one 'moving about in worlds unrealized.' It seemed to be trying to comprehend a curiosity which it had good reason to believe might be a new danger. I almost felt a tenderness for it, and never have*

I experienced such a minute in my life. Down in my room I had a camera and a rifle. Yet I was the only one on the bridge besides the quartermaster at the wheel. I don't mind confessing that I wavered between my duty and my desire for some kind of a

shot. Finally I stayed, but I don't know whether I should take full credit for that or not because I hated to lose sight of the thing. As it watched me it churned the water into foam and spray with its huge front fins. As it went out of sight it emitted a piercing wail like that of a baby. Its voice was altogether out of proportion to its size.

During the First World War, in 1915, the Commander of a German V.28 submarine, Georg Gunther Freiherr von Forstner, and his crew had the following experience (as reported several years later in a newspaper):

On 30 July 1915 our V.28 torpedoed the British steamer 'Iberian' (5,223 tons) carrying a rich cargo in the North Atlantic. The steamer, which was about 600 feet long, sank quickly, the bow sticking almost vertically into the air, towards the bottom a thousand fathoms or more below. When the steamer had been gone for about 25 seconds, there was a violent explosion at a depth which it was clearly impossible for us to know, but which we can reckon, without risking being far out, at about 500 fathoms. A little later pieces of wreckage, and among them a gigantic sea-animal, writhing and struggling wildly, were ejected out of the water to a height of 60 to 100 feet.

At that moment I had with me in the conning tower two officers of the watch, the chief engineer, the navigator, and the helmsman. We at once centered our attention upon this wonder of the seas. As it was not in Brockhaus nor in Brehm we were, alas, unable to identify it. We did not have the time to take a photograph, for the animal sank out of sight after 10 to 15 seconds. It was about 60 feet long, was like a crocodile in shape and had four limbs with powerful webbed feet and a long tail tapering to a point.

That the animal should have been driven up from a great depth seemed to me very understandable. After the explosion, however it was caused, the 'undersea crocodile' as we called it, was shot upwards by the terrific pressure until it leapt out of the water gasping and terrified.

It seems surprising that more sea-serpents were not reported in the North Atlantic during the war years, but these are the last things for which ship's eyes would be scanning the sea's surface. It is a fact, however, that the British Navy claims many more sightings of submarines in these waters than German records show were actually there. This is the territory of the many-humped and long-necked sea-serpents. Many sea-serpent witnesses have likened them to "periscopes" or "telephone poles" sticking out of the water; it seems possible, therefore, that these could actually account for some of the "missing" submarines!

chapter nine

SEA-SERPENTS - WEST COAST.

IN OCTOBER, 1933, THERE WAS A new report of a sea-serpent from the other side of Canada - the Straits of Georgia, between Vancouver Island and the mainland of British Columbia. This sighting, the first to be reported on Canada's west coast, was by the Clerk to the British Columbia legislature, Major W. H. Langley, who was also a barrister and a person of considerable integrity.

On Sunday (1st October 1933) my wife and I went for a sail in the Dorothy *around Discovery and Chatham Islands. It was a beautiful sunny day, with a nice northerly breeze. On entering the passage between the north end of Chatham Island and Fulford Reef, the breeze lightened a bit, and we were proceeding almost on an even keel, with the end of the floodtide under us, when the incident happened which for brevity's sake, is set out in the following numbered paragraphs: 1. - The time was about 1.30 p.m. 2. - We were proceeding quite slowly and silently when my attention was attracted by a very loud noise, something between a grunt and a snort accompanied by a huge hiss. 3. - I looked ahead in the direction of the noise, at the same time shouting at my wife, and we both saw a huge object about 90 to 100 feet off, a little on the port bow, and on the edge of the kelp just off the Chatham Island shore. It was only visible for a few seconds, but what both of us are absolutely agreed upon may be put down as follows: (a) It was every bit as big as the back of a large whale, but entirely different in many respects. (b) Its*

The Sea Hag. Courtesy of the Provincial Archives, Victoria, B.C.

colour was . . . a sort of dark olive green. It had markings along the top and sides. They seemed to be of a serrated nature. 4. - Its colour was very distinct, as the sun was shining brightly on its wetted surface, and it was such a short distance away that there could be no mistaking it. 5. - Just shortly after it went down a swirl appeared on the surface of the water ahead of the Dorothy. 6. - My wife saw it break water a very short time afterwards on the other side of Fulford Reef. The appearance was exactly similar, but it was much farther away and had travelled fast. 7. - The only part of it that we saw was a huge dome of what was apparently a portion of its back.

I may add that I have been cruising about local waters for nearly forty years in my leisure time. I have seen dozens of black-fish. A boat I was in, in 1911, killed three whales - a hump-back, sulphur bottom, and fin-back and towed them alongside to the whaling station at Sechart. Upon arrival at the station there was a sperm whale hauled out there. There was no similarity except in size between any of these and the creature we saw on Sunday. A porpoise, of course, would look like a sprat in comparison with it. Upon comparing notes with Mr. Kemp, the appearance of this object tallies almost exactly with the creature that he and others saw about a year ago in the same neighbourhood.

As in the case of other Canadian monsters, sea-serpent sightings were often not reported until years later, when, after learning of another report, previous witnesses were prompted to come forward and tell their own stories. Fear of being laughed at is a very strong deterrent to people speaking out.

After learning of Major Langley's report, Mr. F. W. Kemp, an officer of the Provincial Archives, told of his experience the year before. This is his report, as given to the *Victoria Daily Times:*

On August 10, 1932, I was with my wife and son on Chatham Island in the Strait of Juan de Fuca. My wife called my attention to a mysterious something coming through the channel between Strong Tide Island and Chatham Island. Imagine my astonishment on observing a huge creature with head out of the water travelling about four miles per hour against the tide. Even at that speed a considerable wash was thrown on the rocks, which gave me the impression that it was more reptile than serpent to make so much displacement.

The channel at this point is about 500 yards wide. Swimming to the steep rocks of the Island opposite, the creature shot its head out of the water on to the rock, and moving its head from side to side, appeared to be taking its bearings. Then fold after fold of its body came to the surface. Towards the tail it appeared serrated with something moving flail-like at the extreme end.

The movements were like those of a crocodile. Around the head appeared a sort of mane, which drifted round the body like kelp.

The Thing's presence seemed to change the whole landscape, which makes it difficult to describe my experiences. It did not seem to belong to the present scheme of things, but rather to the Long Ago when the world was young. The position it held *on the rock was momentary. My wife and sixteen-year-old son ran to a point of land to get a clearer view. I think the sounds they made disturbed the animal. The sea being very calm, it seemed to slip back into deep water; there was a great commotion under the surface and it disappeared like a flash.*

In my opinion its speed must be terrific and its senses of smell, sight and hearing developed to a very high degree. It would be terribly hard to photograph, as its movements are different from anything I have ever seen or heard of. I should say its length to be not less than 80 feet. There were some logs on Strong Tide Island which gave me a good idea as to the size of the monster as it passed them. I took a measurement of one the next day which was over 60 feet in length, and the creature overlapped it to a large extent at each end. I put a newspaper on the spot where it rested its head and took an observation from our previous point of vantage. The animal's head was very much larger than the double sheet of newspaper. The body must have been at least 5 feet thick, and was of a bluish-green colour which shone in the sun like aluminium. I could not determine the shape of the head, but it was much thicker than the body.

I did not report my strange adventure except to one or two trusted friends, for fear of ridicule and unbelief. About a year later, it fell to Major W. H. Langley's lot to see the same or at any rate, a similar monster in the vicinity also of Chatham Island.

Although a year apart, these two sightings would seem to be of the same animal.

Within a week of publication of the Langley report, Archie Willis, the news editor of the *Victoria Daily Times,* had "a dozen letters from other people who said they had seen the serpent, but had refrained from saying anything about it for fear of ridicule." One such case was that of "Rusty" Beetle of Port Angeles, Vancouver Island, who had seen the animal some years before. It seemed the sea-serpent appeared close to "Rusty's" boat while he was fishing off Dungeness Spit in Juan de Fuca Strait. The animal was serpentine and had a body at least forty feet long. The head was like that of a camel or horse and there was a mane. It swam slowly round the boat for five to ten minutes. When "Rusty" came ashore he excitedly related the incident to the boat's owner, who replied: "Rusty, it isn't smart to take a bottle along with you when you go out fishing by yourself." Disappointed that the boat owner did not believe him, "Rusty" then told the story to a local journalist he knew well, but the response was the same. "Rusty" had then decided to keep quiet about the matter.

By now Archie Willis had found a name for the animal - *Cadborosaurus,* after Cadboro Bay, where it was first seen, and after Cadboro, a beautiful legendary Indian maiden. Cadboro was so lovely that the gods decreed she should remain untouched by man. A young and reckless Indian brave named Saurus defied the gods and wooed her. The angry god of air and water took his revenge by turning himself into an eagle and carrying off Cadboro. He punished her by turning her into a stone - reputedly, Gonzales Hill. Saurus was transformed into a sea-serpent and was banished to the depths of the ocean for a billion years.

Reports of the sea-serpent began to come in fast and furiously. Some were obvious hoaxes, but Willis weeded them out and accepted only signed, verifiable reports. In the end he had a list of nearly one hundred persons who had seen the monster.

On October 4th, 1933, the animal was again seen near Chatham Island by a well known yachtsman named R. C. Ross. Excitement ran high. "Have you seen Caddy?" people asked each other as they met on the streets, and the newspapers echoed the cry. And as the white man's excitement grew, a smile touched the lips of the Chinook Indian. The *Cadborosaurus* was not new to him - he had been familiar with *Hiachuckaluck* for centuries!

It was hard to believe that the same animal could have survived for hundreds of years; there must be others - perhaps families and generations of them!

Then another monster was seen in the same area. "This must be Caddy's mate," said the romantics of Victoria, who promptly christened her "Amy." She was a little smaller than Caddy, brownish-grey, with a horselike head. If the animal had eyes they were very small and not noticeable. There were also no ears, mane, whiskers or moustache - as befits a lady.

The differences between these two monsters was probably not due to sex, but to the fact that they were different types of sea-serpents. Amy was of the long-necked variety and Caddy was a merhorse. The people of Victoria became very fond of their monsters, and described them as "loveable and homely" and with "warm and kindly eyes."

Toward the end of 1934 a carcase was found rotting on the beach at Henry Island, British Columbia. It measured thirty feet long, and had reddish flesh and skin covered with hair mixed with quills. The head resembled that of a horse. Attached to the spinal column were what looked like four fins or flippers. The carcase was hauled up on the quay at Prince Rupert where it was examined and photographed. Some of these photographs appeared in the *Illustrated London News* on 15th December, 1934. In the opinion of the Director of the Dominion Experimental Fisheries Station, Dr. Neal Carter, the remains were clearly those of a mammal and "in life it must have been slender and sinewy."

Could this have been one of Caddy's relatives, people wondered? But after careful examination and study of the skull and parts at the Government Biological Station at Nanaimo, B.C., the director, Dr. Clements, pronounced the remains to be those of a basking-shark.

In 1937 came the report of the monster seen by Mr. and Mrs. Timeus, at Sunset Beach, twenty-two miles north of Vancouver. This monster turned out to be a Northern Sea-elephant, one of the strangest and largest mammals in the sea. A sea-serpent was seen, however, at Sunset Bay later that year by two brothers, acquaintances of the Timeuses, Fred and George Lawrence. The animal had a head like a camel's, a small neck, and a body about the size of a large barrel. It was between fifty and sixty feet long. A similar monster had been seen nearby by several fishermen, who judged its length to be closer to one hundred feet.

"K.D." Courtesy of the Provincial Archives, Victoria, B.C.

chapter ten

*VANCOUVER ISLAND'S RESIDENT
SEA-SERPENT: FACT OR FANCY?*

THROUGHOUT THE SECOND WORLD

war there was little mention of sea-serpents - it seemed everyone was too busy fighting the war to notice them. But Caddy did come up from his watery home long enough to be seen in April, 1942, off Estevan Point. Later in the year, when a Japanese submarine shelled this desolate site, it was the opinion of the local fishermen that the enemy had been firing at Caddy, mistaking him for a new Canadian secret weapon!

Ernest Lee, skipper of a motor fishing boat, claimed in the spring of 1943 that he had rammed Caddy twice off Vancouver Island, and that the creature had "sunk to rise no more." The people of Victoria were shocked and indignant. This was declared a very wicked deed! But their fears were unfounded as Caddy was shortly seen again, frolicking in his very own, oversized fishtank - the Sound.

In 1946 monster reports came in again, this time from the Gulf of Georgia. Captain House of the Canadian Government Fishery Patrol saw a monster looking "like a thirty foot telephone pole" near Hecate Strait, between Queen Charlotte Islands and the mainland. Mr. A. K. McMartin of Vancouver suggested a syndicate be formed to capture the monster and that it should be exhibited in the city's swimming pool, as part of Vancouver's celebrations of the founding of the city. But his suggestion was not received kindly, particularly by animal lovers who remembered Caddy's "warm and kindly eyes," and so nothing further came of the suggestion.

In March, 1947, a monster was seen near Siwash Rock by Peter

Pantages, a Greek who ran a restaurant in Vancouver, and by a taxidriver named Oscar.

In the following November, George W. Saggers, a fisherman from Ucleulet on Vancouver Island, saw the monster while he was salmon fishing. The following account, perhaps over-dramatized, appeared in the American magazine *Fate:*

> *Suddenly I had the funniest feeling. A sort of shiver went up and down my spine, and I had a feeling that I was being watched. Immediately I looked all around.*

"Sea-serpent" of Henry Island, B.C., 1934 (a basking shark). Courtesy Public Archives Canada

> *On the port side, about 150 feet away, was a head and neck raised about four feet above the water, with two jet black eyes about three inches across and protruding from the head like buns, staring at me.*
>
> *It just didn't look real. I've never seen anything like it. The head seemed to be the same size as the neck, about eighteen inches through and of a mottled colour of gray and light brown . . .*
>
> *After it looked at me for one full minute, it turned its head straight away from me, showing the back of its head and neck. It appeared to have some sort of mane, which seemed like bundles of warts rather than hair. It looked something like a mattress would, if split down the middle allowing rolls of cotton batting*

to protrude. The colour of the mane was dark brown.

This monster sounds enough like Caddy to be a relative, or was Caddy himself visiting other waters?

Also in 1947 there were *Cadborosaurus* sightings off the icy shores of Alaska - in Security Bay and near the north point of Pennock Island.

In November, 1947, the remains of a huge animal were found on the rocky shore of Vancouver Island near Effingham. Henry Schwarz, a timber merchant and fisherman from Alberni, had made the discovery as he was hauling in his fishing nets. The head was the size of a sheep's

Courtesy Public Archives Canada

and was attached to a spinal column forty feet long. The people of Victoria were very apprehensive. Had Ernest Lee's bragging been true after all? Was Caddy dead?

With the help of two lumbermen and the skipper of the fishing boat *Dana*, Schwarz was able to transport the remains - in two sections, leaving the tail piece in the water - to Alberni, where they were exhibited to the public. There was a skull, one foot two inches long and eight and a half inches wide, and one hundred and forty-five cylindrical vertebrae - the largest six inches in diameter and the smallest one and a half inches.

After much examination and discussion by experts, it was finally stated that the remains were probably those of a basking-shark in the last stages of decay.

Victoria breathed again! Their beloved Caddy was safe!

In 1950 there were two more reports of sea-serpents off Victoria. One was by Judge Thomas Brown, President of the King's Bench of Saskatchewan, who was vacationing with his family in Victoria; the other by the acting postmistress of a small resort called Summerland. The lady's report generally agrees with others given of Caddy. She watched it for about ten minutes.

During 1948, 1949, and 1950, sea-serpent sightings were extremely numerous. On February 13th, 1953, Caddy entertained ten people who watched from different points of view as he swam in Qualicum Bay for more than an hour. In February, 1954, about thirty people watched him basking on the surface some way from shore at Nanaimo.

Near the end of April, 1958, a small sea-serpent was seen off Whidbey Island in Pudget Sound, sixty miles from Vancouver. Rev. John Oosterhoff, of Mount Vernon Presbyterian Church, and several other people saw the monster. Its undulations made it hard to observe, but they estimated it was twelve feet long and one foot thick. Was this a baby *Cadborosaurus?*

Caddy entertained again on 19th July, 1959, while a whole family from Victoria were fishing from two boats near Race Rocks. His jagged dorsal crest cut through the water at considerable speed, delighting his audience of nine-year-old Greg Cameron, his father, two uncles and grandfather.

Caddy made another appearance on Boxing Day, 1960. A Sidney couple were attracted by clouds of seagulls which seemed to be diving at something in the water about half a mile off shore. Head raised eight feet out of water, Caddy was speeding southwards.

Another strange animal, that doesn't seem to fit any previous sea-serpent report, appeared in British Columbian waters in 1962. This creature was seen first by a Mrs. MacLean from her country house on Campbell River, Vancouver Island. Her husband saw it too when he came home, and at once phoned his friend Ted Smitheringale. Before Ted could arrive, however, two fishermen, mistaking the creature for a sea-lion, shot at it and it disappeared. According to Mrs. MacLean's description the animal was eighteen feet long and had a big hump on its back, which rose above the water. Its body was creamy yellow and was streaked with red veins. At the extreme end the body ended with a darker "ball." For about fifteen minutes the Macleans watched the animal wallowing in the floating seaweed. One wonders how the fishermen could have mistaken such an animal for a sea-lion, but, as Mr. Maclean said, they were at sea-level and could not have seen it as well as he and his wife, who were some forty feet above.

We shall never know quite what sort of sea-monster this was. It could have been something altogether new, or it could have been a *Cadborosaurus* "in abnormal condition - sick or moulting," as Dr. Bernard Heulvelmans suggests in his book *In the Wake of the Sea-Serpents.* But whatever it was, it certainly lacked Caddy's appeal.

Poor Alan Maclean probably regretted ever reporting the monster.

He received a flood of mail which included invitations to speak at a forthcoming Liar's Congress, a card offering him honourary life membership in Alcoholics Anonymous and a number of offers to have his eyes tested free of charge.

On October 9th, 1969, *The Daily Times* carried the following article.

"IS CADBOROSAURUS ALL TALE?"
Not So, Say Secretive Callers.

What Victoria needs is a Sea-Serpent Society. For the protection of the members, meetings should be held in camera.

The need was confirmed Wednesday when I received a barrage of phone calls backing up Cadboro Bay residents' belief the creature they saw gambolling around the bay that morning was a pint-sized version of Caddy, the sea serpent who had haunted our water since at least 1928.

Several of the callers said they had seen Caddy themselves. All of them wished to remain anonymous.

I don't blame them. Who wants to run the risk of having his neighbors think he's ready for the funny farm?

The article went on to say one caller to the newpaper thought sea-serpents would have a natural affinity for Cadboro Bay. "Everyone knows the water is warmer there than in the Strait and reptiles gravitate to warmer temperatures."

Another caller deplored the lack of research done on the incubation period and mating habits of sea-serpents. He called it "a deplorable lack in scientific advancement." In his opinion any sea-serpent society should concentrate on study groups.

Caddy put in another appearance in December, 1970. Glenn Bertie, a fourteen-year-old student at Central Junior High School, gave the following report to the *Daily Colonist*:

"I was walking along the beach alone below the Chinese cemetery near Harling Point overlooking Foul Bay.

"I came around a point, and there, about 50 feet away out in the water, was what looked like the head of a giant cobra, about a foot out of the water.

"It was brown, like brown skin and the head was flat on top. I didn't notice any eyes.

"I guess the thing saw me, because it dived right away towards the open water. Then the back of the thing came up out of the water and went back in. There were fins on it. It looked like a giant snake, maybe 20 feet long."

Glen said it couldn't have been a seal, because it was much too big. After the creature dived, he said, he didn't see it again.

Reports of Caddy and other sea-serpents have become less frequent in recent years. Perhaps things have become too "busy" for his liking

The Serpent of Second Narrows. Courtesy of the Provincial Archives, Victoria, B.C.

around Victoria and he and his relatives have moved on to quieter places. Perhaps he is just off on a goodwill visit to other waters. But no doubt he will be in the news again shortly.

In the meantime, the sea-serpent's existence will continue to be one of conjecture until such time as a carcase or some other remains are found and identified conclusively.

I must confess, I believe in sea-serpents - perhaps because Caddy's lovable nature intrigues my imagination. I like the idea of this homely monster coming up from the caverns of the deep every so often, just to have a look round and see how we're getting along.

An interesting fact has been observed. When goldfish are introduced into the Great Lakes, they grow to enormous size, in keeping with their environment. It seems possible that the same process could occur with any kind of creature living in the sea. Their tendency, in the interests of maneuverability as their size increases, would be to elongate and become serpentine. As Ivan Sanderson wrote in his book *Follow the Whale*:

> There presumably is no limit to size in oceans, but there probably are limitations on form as one moves up in length. If there are two hundred foot creatures as yet undiscovered in the sea, they will probably prove to be greatly elongated or serpentine in form, whether they be seals, whales, or other mammals, or even fish.

This being the case, any of the above creatures, if overgrown and serpentine could be classified as sea-serpents. Their lithe forms and exceptional speeds would help to keep their existence secret longer than other smaller species.

What is man doing today to solve the fascinating sea-serpent mystery? Several things. Attempts are being made to catch a sea-serpent. This is difficult enough to do in places like Lake Okanagan, let alone in the sea. Even today vast areas of the sea wastes lie uncharted.

Prof. John D. Isaacs, Director of Marine Life Research at the Scripps Institution of Oceanography, La Jolla, California, is working on various kinds of traps to catch large, little-known sea animals. One of these traps is like a huge circular net several hundred feet wide, weighted in the centre and with floats around the edge. The weight would be discharged at a certain depth, and then the net-acting like a parachute in reverse — would rise to the surface scooping up everything large and small in its path.

Modern technology has provided the tools for man to make great sea journeys and explorations. Captain Jacques-Yves Cousteau, Director of the Oceanographic Museum of Monaco, developed the aqualung which enables man to explore the upper layer of the sea to a depth of one hundred and eighty feet (thirty fathoms). His little bright-yellow, two-man diving saucer, or "Souscoupe" — the first of the Deepstar family of submersibles — can easily explore depths to twelve hundred feet. The largest Deepstar can explore to twenty thousand feet and the U.S. Navy's bathyscaphe "Trieste" to thirty-six thousand feet. These are only some of the deep submergence vehicles equipped with movie cameras and television, or "eyes" with which to search the ocean depths for unknown sea-creatures.

Drawbacks to the effective use of motor-driven observation devices lie in their noisy approach and gleaming searchlights which warn off sea creatures.

Another Cousteau project, a fixed oceanographic station, might be a more successful means of solving the riddle of the sea-serpent. One of these stations, or laboratory buoys, is situated halfway between Corsica and the mainland. Designed to continuously observe life under the sea to a depth of one hundred and fifty feet, it resembles a gigantic needle or watertight tube, two hundred and twenty-seven feet long, floating vertically in the water. Only the top is above the surface, the tube being anchored to the ocean floor with nylon or polypropylene cables.

With the increased use of television and movie cameras by deepsea commercial engineering concerns, mysteries of the deep are constantly being revealed. Not long ago a strange and puzzling "monster" suddenly appeared on an underwater television system in the control cabin of a Shell Oil drilling vessel off Santa Barbara, California. It was recorded permanently from the screen on movie film. The creature, nicknamed "Marvin," appears as a fifteen foot whitish mass with ridges spiralling around its body. Scientists at the University of Texas believe it is an unknown creature that may or may not have changed since prehistoric times.

Could it have been a small sea-serpent? We shall never know — but with constant improvements in underwater photographic equipment, such pictures will eventually appear as clear-cut images, which leave no doubt as to their subject. In time modern technology should reveal all the "monsters" that actually exist — on land and under the sea. Then zoologists and marine biologists will record them as clear-cut facts.

Monsters? Yes, Canada has her share. Next time you visit a quiet, deep lake keep your eyes open. You might be lucky enough to see one of *Ogopogo's* relatives — or there is always lovable, homely "Caddy," on the West Coast. But I wouldn't suggest you go searching around Harrison Lake for that other kind of monster — the wildman, or *Sasquatch.* He plays rough!

my personal sighting record

THE GREAT SEA SERPENT
(according to Pontoppidan)

Life-sized dinosaur, Prehistoric Zoo, Calgary, Alberta. Photo courtesy
Information Canada Photothèque

Bibliography

Bartley, Allan. "Monster or Muskrat." *The Ottawa Citizen,* June 8, 1976.

Beck, Horace. *Folk Lore and the Sea.* Middleton, Connecticut: Wesleyan University Press, 1973.

Benton, William. "Sea Serpent." *The New Encyclopedia Britannica Micropedia,* (1974 ed.) IX, 10.

Boggs, R.S. "Sea Serpents." *Merit Students Encyclopedia,* (1967 ed.) XVI, 496-497.

Bourguignon, Erika. *Encyclopedia Americana,* (1975 ed.) XII, 727.

Burns, J. "My Search for British Columbia's Giant Indians." *Liberty,* (December, 1954).

Byrne, Peter. *The Search for Bigfoot, Monster, Myth or Man?* Washington: Acropolis Books Limited, 1975.

_____ . and Celia Killeen. *Bigfoot News,* (June 1975), VIII. Editorial.

"Caddy the Sea Serpent Sighted by Student." *Daily Colonist,* Victoria. December, 1970, p. 45.

"Caddy Visits Foul Bay?" *Victoria Daily Times,* December 14, 1970.

Clark, Eugenie. *The Lady and the Sharks.* New York: Harper and Row, 1969.

Clarke, John. "Dark Monster from the Deep. Ogopogo." *The Globe and Mail,* July 31, 1976. p. 8.

Cocking, Clive. "The Magical, Mystical, Mythical Sasquatch." *Weekend Magazine,* (May 10, 1975).

Colbert, Edwin H. *Men and Dinosaurs, The Search in Field and Laboratory.* New York: E.P. Dutton and Co. Inc., 1968.

Cousteau, Jacques-Yves. *World Without Sun.* New York: Harper and Row, 1964.

Cromie, W.J. *The Living World of the Sea.* Toronto: Prentice-Hall of Canada, 1966.

Dewdney, Selwyn, and Kidd, Kenneth E. *Indian Rock Paintings of the Great Lakes.* University of Toronto Press, 1967.

Dickie, F. "Cave Men in British Columbia?" *Toronto Star Weekly* (July 21, 1934).

Dinsdale, Tim. *Monster Hunt,* Washington: Acropolis Books Limited, 1972.

_____ . *The Leviathans.* London: Routledge and K. Paul, 1966.

"Diving Saucer." *The New Book of Knowledge.* New York: Grolier Inc., (1974 ed.) XIX, 18.

Drew, Wayland and others. *The Nature of Fish.* National Science of Canada Limited, Jack McClelland, 1974.

Dufour, Pat. "Is Cadborosaurus All Tale? Not So, Say Secretive Callers." *Victoria Daily Times,* October 9, 1969. p. 21.

Folgelson, Raymond D. "Windigo." *Encyclopedia Americana,* (1975 ed.) XXIX, 22.

Franklin, Stephen. "The Trail of the Sasquatch," *Weekend Magazine,* IX (November 14, 1959).

"Giant 'Sasquatch' prints found in Skeena Area." *Northern Times,* August 20, 1976.

Gould, Rupert T. *The Case for the Sea-Serpent.* Detroit: Singing Tree Press, 1969.

Green, John. *On the Track of the Sasquatch.* Agassiz, B.C.; Cheam Publishing Limited, 1968.

_____ . *The Sasquatch File.* Agassiz, B.C.: Cheam Publishing Limited, 1973.

Hamlyn, Paul. *Larousse Encyclopedia of Animal Life.* England: The Hamlyn Publishing Group Limited, 1971.

Helm, Thomas. *Monsters of the Deep.* New York: Dodd Mead and Company, 1962.

Heuvelmans, Bernard. *In The Wake of the Sea-Serpents.* London: Rupert Hart-Davis, 1968.

Holiday, F.W. *The Great Orm of Loch Ness.* London: Faber and Faber, 1968.

Hunt, Alison. "The West Coast's Abominable Treemen." *The Globe Magazine,* (July 6, 1957).

Hunter, Don with Dahinden, Rene. *Sasquatch.* Toronto: McClelland and Stewart, 1973.

"Irishman Devotes His Life to Seeking Elusive Bigfoot." *The Los Angeles Times,* reprinted in *The Globe and Mail,* December 15, 1975.

Kovalik, Vladimir, and Nada. *The Ocean World.* New York: Holiday House, 1966.

"Lake monster lives in memory and murk." (CP) *The Hamilton Spectator,* October 6, 1976.

Lyell, Sir Charles. *A Second Visit to the United States of North America.* London: Scholarly Press, 1849.

Mathews, Leonard Harrison and others. *The Whale.* New York: Simon and Shuster, 1968.

McCormick, Harold. *Shadows in the Sea.* Philadelphia: Chilton Book Company, 1970.

McNulty, Faith. *Whales: Their Life in the Sea.* New York: Harper and Row, 1975.

Morris, Byron. "Egad, It's a Denizen of the Deep." *Weekend Magazine,* (December 2, 1972).

"Mysterious Footprints." *The New Book of Knowledge Annual,* (1975 ed.), 154. New York: Grolier Incorporated.

Napier, John. *Bigfoot*. England: Reader's Union Limited, 1972.

──────────── . *The Yeti and Sasquatch in Myth and Reality,* London: Cape, 1972.

O'Connor, Patrick Fitzgerald. *Shark-O!* London: Secker and Warburg, 1953.

"Ogopogo Sighted." *The Globe and Mail,* July 9, 1976, p. 9.

Perry, Richard. *The Unknown Ocean.* New York: Taplinger Publishing Company, 1972.

Picton, John. "Sasquatch Officially Recognised." *The Globe and Mail,* September 24, 1975.

Place, Marian T. *On The Track of Bigfoot.* New York: Dodd, Mead and Company, 1974.

Quinn, Daniel. *Land and Sea Monsters.* Northbrook, Illinois: Hubbard Press, 1971.

Ross, Frank Jr. *Undersea Vehicles and Habitats.* New York: Thomas Y. Crowell Company, 1970.

Sanderson, Ivan. *Follow the Whale.* Boston and Toronto: Little Brown and Company, 1956.

"Sasquatch." *Encyclopedia Canadiana,* (1975 ed.), IX, 233.

"Sasquatch sighting has Kimberley wondering if it's been ad-hoaxed." *The Vancouver Sun,* September 10, 1976.

"Sasquatch." *U.S. Army Corps of Engineers Washington Environmental Atlas,* 1975, page 53.

"Sea-Serpent off Vancouver." *Fate Magazine,* Highland Park, Illinois, (Summer 1948).

Stephen, David. *Dolphins, Seals and Other Sea Mammals, Animal World Series,* New York: G.P. Putnam's Sons, 1973.

Sternberg, C.M. *Canadian Dinosaurs,* National Museum of Canada, Geological Series No. 54. Bulletin 103.

Storey, Tracey. "Sea Serpent." *Encyclopedia Americana,* (1975 ed.) XXIV, 478-479.

Sweeney, James B. *A Pictorial History of Sea Monsters and Other Dangerous Marine Life.* New York: Crown Publishers, 1972.

Swinton, W.E. *Dinosaurs of Canada.* Royal Ontario Museum/University of Toronto, 1965.

Williams, Jerome and others. *Sea and Air.* The Naval Environment. United States Naval Institute, 1968.

"Will This Trap Catch a Sea-Monster?" *Popular Science Monthly,* New York, (October 1959).

"Windigo." *Encyclopedia Canadiana,* (1975 ed.) X, 335.

Wright, Bruce. Director of Northeastern Wildlife Station. "Sasquatchery - To Date!" *The Atlantic Advocate,* (October 1969).

other monsters

LA BALEINE D'OSTENDE.

Visitée par l'Éléphant, la Giraffe & les Osages.